JOANNA LOTT AND RI

YOUR DREAM JOB TOOLKIT

HOW TO LAND A JOB YOU LOVE

Your Dream Job Toolkit

Design and Production: Catherine Williams, Chapter One Book Production

Printed in the United Kingdom

Contents

"Tell me, what is it you plan to do with your one wild and precious life?"

—Mary Oliver

Introduction to
Your Dream Job Toolkit

Why you need this book

The COVID-19 pandemic of 2020-2021 has transformed the world of work for ever. The economic uncertainty has cost many their jobs and livelihoods; others have been driven to work in new ways – for example from home and embracing new technology.

Countless others – such as key workers in the NHS, retail, those who produce and deliver our food, teachers and care home workers – have had no choice but to keep going under sometimes very difficult circumstances.

The upshot is that many people – even those in secure jobs – are reassessing their lives, values, priorities and careers.

Against a background of turmoil for many, this toolkit seeks to help you uncover your unique talents and gifts, so that you can stand out in a sea of candidates and land a role that you want and can excel in, even if you are changing to a new industry or sector.

This toolkit is for you if you:

- are trying to find your true purpose in life
- have been made redundant and need some practical help

- ◆ feel like your career is threatened by Covid-19 and want to consider your options
- ◆ feel unfulfilled and are considering a change of career
- ◆ are trying to figure out whether to start your own business.

The method we offer will help you navigate your job search with ease and confidence, uncover the best of yourself, and use that to take steps to secure your next exciting opportunity. One obstacle is that many of us use only traditional job search approaches. By following this method, you will discover different, proven strategies to make progress and find meaningful, empowering and interesting work.

We've been there

Our combined experience started during the 2009 recession, when we worked with more than 200 individuals, helping them secure fulfilling jobs, and since then through workshops, group programmes and one-to-one coaching. We also have a long history of helping people wanting to set up their own businesses. Our bio notes are at the end of this toolkit.

Career Planning System

We know that many people want to rush the job hunt process by just getting on and applying for jobs, firing off CVs to recruitment agencies, and answering published vacancy adverts. Although you feel that you are keeping busy, this is not necessarily the most effective strategy. Adopting an approach of "slow down to speed up" is more likely to get you interviews and secure a job you want.

The Career Planning System we introduce in Chapter 1 is a well-proven journey, based not only on our experience but that of other career specialists who have adopted this approach.

What we ask of you

We cannot emphasise strongly enough that your competitive edge comes from being aware of and highlighting your unique strengths and talents, maximising the use of the invisible job market, keeping an open mind about potential employers and using social media to the maximum.

We also ask you to commit to the process. Is it easy? Not always. It will take work. Is it possible? Absolutely, YES. We are not talking about half-heartedly pondering the questions while watching TV but focused, consistent action with maximum effort in completing the exercises properly.

Your Dream Job Toolkit is designed as a working toolbox, so make it your own. Consider creating a binder or electronic folder containing all your papers relating to career planning and your job search.

There is no guarantee of how long it takes to get a new job, but you can boost your chances through daily consistency. So, treat it like a project. Carve out a decent block of time every day, or every other day, to focus on this work and you will make significant progress.

What's included

There are 11 steps to work through:

- Chapter 1 – The overall process of changing jobs and securing the job you want
- Chapter 2 – Your unique talents and strengths
- Chapter 3 – Be guided by what you truly value
- Chapter 4 – Personal barriers and self-limiting beliefs
- Chapter 5 – Putting all the pieces together to find a job
- Chapter 6 – The importance of networking for your career
- Chapter 7 – Writing and improving my LinkedIn profile, CV/online applications and covering letters

- Chapter 8 – Preparing for an interview
- Chapter 9 – Presenting well at interviews
- Chapter 10 – Support systems and next steps
- Chapter 11 – Is self-employment for me?

Each chapter covers:
- learning outcomes
- a chapter outline
- exercises
- useful resources.

If you want to continue in a similar role within your current industry, focus first on Chapters 6, 7, 8, and 9. Then work through the other chapters to enrich your networking, job applications and interviews.

If you want to switch to a different job role or a different industry or sector, work through this toolkit in sequence.

Our promise to you

The three shifts that will give you the competitive edge in your job search are:

- knowing how you are unique
- knowing the external needs (including how to navigate the job market)
- maintaining confidence and momentum.

This toolkit offers a structured learning path with 11 steps to move you through these three shifts and get you from feeling anxious about the job market to marketing your best self so that you can successfully secure a job.

Want more help?

For some people, particularly if you complete all the exercises, this toolkit will be enough. Others may want additional help.

Further resources

A checklist and tracker to record your insights from this Toolkit is available at www.joannalottcoaching.com. Additional free exercises and materials will also be added to this website.

Inspiration and content

For inspiration and further resources, you can connect with us on social media:

LinkedIn:
https://www.linkedin.com/in/joannalott/
https://www.linkedin.com/in/richard-fox-a843272/
Instagram:
https://www.instagram.com/joanna_lott_coaching/

Career membership, group coaching programmes and one-to-one coaching

Your job search can be a worrying or lonely time, leaving you feeling anxious and overwhelmed as you consider where to start and how to maintain momentum. If you are job hunting by yourself and would like support, accountability and motivation along the way, we are creating group and one-to-one coaching programmes based on the Career Planning System.

Our approach with the group programmes is to build a community among the participants and provide additional learning, inspiration and support. Visit www.joannalottcoaching.com to learn more.

You can also join our free Facebook community, A Satisfied Mind – https://www.facebook.com/groups/asatisfiedmind

Acknowledgements

We would like to thank you, the reader, for setting aside the time and dedication to commit to working through this book. It demands a lot of energy, and our hope is that it will bring you a rich and fulfilling life.

We wish to thank our respective families for their ongoing support and the "time away" to create and finish this book.

Thank you to freelance sub-editor and journalist Penny Vevers – pennyvevers@hotmail.com – who has polished this book for publication.

> *"You don't have to be great to start, but you have to start to be great."*
>
> —Zig Ziglar

Let's begin.

Chapter 1

The overall process of changing jobs and securing the job you want

"The truth is that our finest moments are most likely to occur when we are feeling deeply uncomfortable, unhappy or unfulfilled. For it is only in such moments, propelled by our discomfort, that we are likely to step out of our ruts and start searching for different ways or truer answers."

—M. Scott Peck

Learning outcomes

By the end of this chapter you will:

- ◆ understand how job vacancies are filled
- ◆ know your options and the various routes you can take
- ◆ begin with the end in mind.

Why this is worth your time

We can't highlight enough why starting with how you are unique is the most effective job hunting method.

Here are some reasons:

1. When you define yourself as a person rather than a job title, you can approach several different markets.
2. You will make better decisions when you know what is important to you.
3. You are constantly growing, learning and evolving. What you loved when you were 21 might not be what you love when you're 50.
4. You can describe exactly what you are looking for when talking to friends/family/other contacts.
5. You will put more energy into the job search when you are searching for something that you want to do.
6. You will be able to approach suitable organisations without waiting for vacancies to be advertised.
7. You will be able to describe to employers what is unique about you.
8. It is a once-in-a lifetime opportunity to pause and think about where you want to go in your life.

Career Planning System

The Career Planning System challenges you to do two types of research:

◆ internal research, which involves exercises to reflect on what is important to you and what you have to offer
◆ external research, which encourages you to look at the job market to see which organisations might be able to offer what you are seeking.

CAREER PLANNING SYSTEM

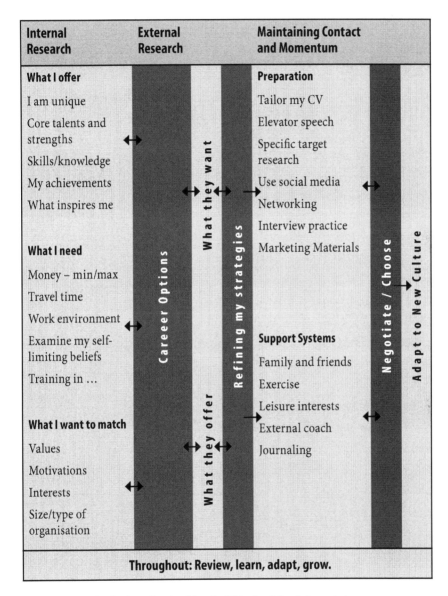

Internal Research	External Research	Maintaining Contact and Momentum
What I offer		**Preparation**
I am unique		Tailor my CV
Core talents and strengths		Elevator speech
Skills/knowledge		Specific target research
My achievements		Use social media
What inspires me		Networking
		Interview practice
What I need		Marketing Materials
Money – min/max		
Travel time		
Work environment		
Examine my self-limiting beliefs		**Support Systems**
Training in …		Family and friends
		Exercise
		Leisure interests
What I want to match		External coach
Values		Journaling
Motivations		
Interests		
Size/type of organisation		

Vertical bands between columns: Career Options · What they want · What they offer · Refining my strategies · Negotiate / Choose · Adapt to New Culture

Throughout: Review, learn, adapt, grow.

Sources include the late Louise Lloyd of Morley Lloyd Associates.

The internal research

Yes, many people are currently looking for a job, but you are unique. The best way to differentiate yourself from the others is to unearth your top three unique talents and strengths. This demands some hard thinking and reflection on who you are and what you want to do with your life. We will walk you through this in Chapter 2.

Be aware that everything that has happened in your life has been preparing you for who you have become. Not a single thing in your life was ever wasted.

You are more than your job title

A lot of us talk about our career as a who we are – "I'm a midwife!" "I'm a teacher!" – but that is a mistake. You are more than your job.

Once you recognise this you can open up limitless possibilities for yourself. When you aren't just tied to one specific job, the world is your oyster, and everything that is important to you will guide you to finding the career that makes the most sense for you. It takes the pressure off having to get things right, and you can focus more on what will make you happy.

The external research

Once you know what you have to offer, you need to do some external research, like into the job market and which organisations might be able to offer what you are seeking.

You will stand a much better chance of getting a job if you allocate 70-80% of your time to focusing on the invisible job market, particularly for a middle to senior role.

The first step is to use your personal and business network and social media contacts to help you get in front of potential employers.

Or you can write directly to the organisations you have researched, explain what you can offer them and back this up with your relevant achievements.

Some organisations post job vacancies on their own websites and often do not use recruitment agencies. We regard these organisations as partially operating in the invisible market, as only a proportion of job applicants look at these websites.

As an absolute maximum, spend 20-30% of your time in the visible job market, ie, join the crowd who sends CVs to recruitment agencies and replies to online adverts.

The visible and invisible job market

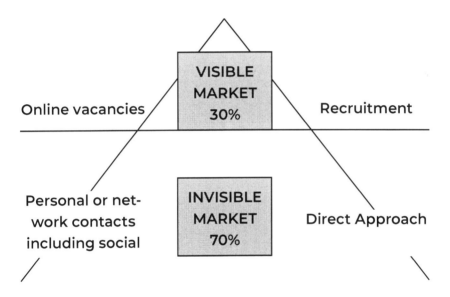

Online vacancies

VISIBLE MARKET 30%

Recruitment

Personal or net-work contacts including social

INVISIBLE MARKET 70%

Direct Approach

Where is work?

Forty years ago, "work" referred to a location where you went every working day of the week. An occasional one day working from home was reserved for senior people. Now "work" is much more about what you do, not where you do it. In some occupations you can successfully carry out your work from virtually anywhere in the world.

If the sort of job you want means you will be required to go into the office nearly every day then, to limit travel time, your future employer is likely to be within a radius of, say, 40km from where you live.

Alternatively, if you will work from home your future employer may be based locally or anywhere else in your country. In fact, if there are skills shortages in another country you may have an opportunity to join an overseas organisation while working from home, or you may choose to relocate. Bear this in mind when you list and research potential employers.

There is still work out there

If you're currently out of work, and looking for a job during the Covid-19 pandemic, you may feel that the situation is rather hopeless given the media is full of the bad news about the unemployment rate climbing. Your situation is not hopeless.

There are whole industries thriving during this pandemic and hiring people right now:

- ◆ *Digital/IT* – anything involving a purely digital product or IT. Roles such as IT professionals, programmers and software engineers are available.
- ◆ *Tech giants* – Google, Facebook, Apple and, of course now, Zoom, are still hiring.
- ◆ *Health* – Doctors, nurses, healthcare assistants, allied health professionals such as physiotherapists and occupational therapists, mental health professionals, vaccinators, pharmacists and many more are all needed.
- ◆ *Financial services* – banking, planning, insurance or accounting are still sought after, with companies such as Fidelity Investments and Capital One currently advertising hundreds of roles at the time of writing.

- *Online/digital education* – online education for both children and adults are in high demand.
- *Supply chain and retail* – while the high street has taken a hammering, online retailers and delivery are on the increase.

Other professions such as insurance, cosmetics, pet breeders and exercise equipment retailers have had huge surges over the pandemic period.

It is worth doing an internet search during your job hunt as whole new areas of the economy may be born and/or revitalised.

EXERCISES

Exercise 1: Your perfectly written novel

This exercise is about looking at every element of your life up to now to guide you into what you want to happen next. You can access a guided contemplation through this exercise on www.joannalott-coaching.com.

Consider asking yourself: "What if every aspect of my life has happened for a reason – even the things that seem random? What if I bring everything about my life into the grand design of what I want to happen next?"

Imagine your life is the perfectly written novel, written by the perfect novelist, where you as the hero/heroine have been put through all these chapters, but not a single chapter was wasted or put there randomly.

Determining the chapters

Divide your age by 10. If you're 40, 40 divided by 10 is 4. If you're 50, 50 divided by 10 is 5. And then multiply that number by 2. So, if you're 40 it becomes 8. If you're 50, it becomes 10.

Basically, you are coming up with five periods of your life, with each one becoming its own chapter, ending with a final chapter set in current times.

So if you're aged 40, the first chapter will be from when you were born until you were 8 years old; if you're 50 it will be from when you were born until you were 10 years old, and so on…

As you work through each chapter, spend a few minutes journaling your key insights. Specifically, for each chapter, document the key gifts of **knowledge**, **strengths** or other gifts that could now contribute to who you are becoming and the **impact** you will be having.

If possible, give the book and each chapter a title.

Chapter 1

Bring together the highlights. What were the most formative aspects of this first chapter of your life? What were the big things that happened – you could include aspects of your parenting and upbringing, starting school, or any other experiences that matter to you. If you had a traumatic experience, there is no need to go into depth – just notice.

And now, importantly, begin to ask yourself: What were the gifts of that chapter that you can potentially bring into your life now, in terms of your **goals and purpose**?

What were the gifts in terms of **knowledge** that you gained? Or **strengths** that you built as a result of this chapter that might help you moving forward. What did you **learn** about yourself or your **impact** on others or life?

Is there a name to this chapter that speaks to you?

Chapter 2

Now move to the second chapter of your life. So, if you are 40 years old, that would be the next 8 years of your life, from 8 to 16. Again, what were the highlights? What were the formative things – the most memorable things – that affected you? And that affect you to this day?

And as you remember, begin to wonder: What are the gifts of that chapter for who you get to be today and the impact you have? These could be gifts of **knowledge**: What did you **learn** about yourself, others, life, world? Or what **strengths** did you grow as a result of the experiences of that chapter? Or, anything else that could be gifts relating to your **goals and purpose**; or the **impact** you have on others in your life.

If your mind comes up blank, that's fine. If your mind gets distracted, going back and forth, that's fine. Don't judge yourself.

Is there a name to this chapter that speaks to you?

Chapters 3-4

Repeat the above

Chapter 5

This chapter brings you up to the point of the coronavirus (Covid-19) pandemic. Use it to get you from where you left off in Chapter 4 to the **beginning** of the pandemic. For example, if you're 40, this chapter will be from age 32 to March 2020, when the virus first struck in the UK.

What were the formative things that happened for you or to you in the run up to the pandemic?

What are the gifts of that chapter for who you get to be? The gifts of **knowledge**? What you **learned**? Or the gifts of **strength** and power that it helped you build? Or anything else that you get to bring into who you are and how and who you might **impact**.

Final chapter

And now, let's do the coronavirus chapter – what you have been experiencing since the pandemic struck? Ask yourself: what are the knowledge/learning or strengths or any other circumstances – as a result of coronavirus – that can be gifts for you? What are the gifts for who you get to be or who you **impact** and how?

The movie and the next book...

Finally, imagine yourself as an audience member watching the perfectly produced movie based on this perfectly written novel. The hero/heroine in this movie is you. Watch everything you have gone through, how it has happened for a reason. This is what has been preparing the hero/heroine for what comes next. And, as an audience member what do you expect happens next for them?

What should happen naturally, organically, as a result of everything that this hero/heroine has been through? What is worthy of all this preparation?

Gently reflect on that. Who does this hero/heroine get to be? What do they get to do? All of this preparation. All of this beautiful past. How do they/you step into this next chapter?

What about the impact you will have? Who might you have that impact on? How powerful is it?

Thanks and credit to Shirzad Chamine for this exercise: https://www.positiveintelligence.com

Useful resources

Books
- *Creating a Purposeful Life* by Richard Fox; Infinite Ideas Limited – The Career Planning System and some of the exercises included here are taken from this book
- *What Color Is Your Parachute?* by Richard Nelson Bolles; Ten Speed Press
- *Build Your Own Rainbow* by Barrie Hopson and Mike Scally; Management Books 2000 Ltd

- *The 7 Habits of Highly Effective People* by Stephen R. Covey; Simon & Schuster – a great personal development book
- *Your Best Year Yet* by Jinny Ditzler; Harper Collins
- *The Squiggly Career* by Helen Tupper and Sarah Ellis; Portfolio Penguin.

Website

- www.positiveintelligence.com – a six-week mental fitness programme to help handle life's great challenges without mental stress or other negative emotions. Co-author Joanna Lott is a pioneer of this programme in the UK.

Chapter 2

Your unique talents and strengths

"Don't ask what the world needs. Ask what makes you come alive and go and do it. Because what the world needs is people who have come alive."

—*Howard Thurman*

Learning outcomes

By the end of this chapter you will:

◆ know your top three unique talents and strengths and how to use these in your job search
◆ have identified your other main skills (learned behaviours) that you want to carry forward to your next job.

You are unique

You have unique fingerprints, eyes, ear lobes and DNA. The information and knowledge you have accumulated over your lifetime are unique to you. Even more relevant to your job search is that you have two or three unique talents and strengths.

If you want to live a fulfilling life, we suggest that you unearth your top talents and strengths and use them to the full, ideally in the service of others, be that with work colleagues, customers and family, as well as in society.

Why do we use the word "unearth"? Because we did not know our own unique talents and strengths until we carried out our own internal research. Furthermore, we discovered that when we talked to clients about this, most of them could have filled two pages with all the things they could do, but they could not answer the question: "What are your top talents and strengths?" It is unlikely that you know what they are.

The value of knowing your strengths and talents

Imagine you are going to an interview tomorrow. How confident would you be in answering questions such as:

◆ What are you really good at doing?
◆ What would you say are your top two or three strengths?
◆ What sort of work really interests you?

We strongly encourage you to invest time in unearthing your top talents and strengths so that you can:

◆ stand out from the crowd
◆ identify the types of jobs in which you would flourish
◆ refer to your unique talents and strengths when networking, writing the personal statement in your CV and answering questions authentically at interviews.

Difference between talent/strength, knowledge and skill

Talent/strength – a personal talent, quality or attribute you possess and have demonstrated

Knowledge – specific knowledge or information necessary in a particular situation, not just generally for your job

Skill – the ability to do something requiring acquired knowledge or a learned behaviour (eg riding a bicycle).

EXERCISES

The following exercises are the most important part of your internal research as you work through The Career Planning System. We encourage you to invest in the time to complete them, as they provide a chance to crystallise your unique talents and strengths and list your other top skills.

Exercise 1 – All about you

Answer the following questions about yourself:

1. What were my favourite childhood pastimes/hobbies?

2. Nowadays, what do I really enjoy doing?

3. What activities am I engaged in when I am at my very best?

4. What activities energise me and make me feel that the "real me" is doing them?

5. What can I learn or do easily that others find more difficult?

6. What do others say I am good at or regard me as an expert in?

7. What are my top 30-50 achievements/things that I was proud of at the time, from all aspects of my life, from childhood onwards?

8. What particular knowledge and skills did I use to achieve 7?

9. Which of these achievements gave me the greatest joy?

10. When I have a list of tasks to do, which one(s) do I do first because I enjoy them?

11. What tasks do I avoid?

12. What talents/parts of myself would I love to use, but haven't yet had the chance to employ?

13. What aspects of my character do I want to use more of in the future?

14. Summary: What topics or themes emerge from the above exercise?

Exercise 2 – Talents and strengths

Review the following list of talents and strengths. Be very selective in marking the items that really describe you. Add any others that are not on the list.

Talents and strengths

Accurate	Achiever	Adaptable	Administration
Advisor	Ambitious	Analyser	Analytical
Assembler	Assertive	Brave	Builder
Calm	Caring	Cheerful	Clarifier
Collaborative	Communicator	Competitive	Completer
Confident	Conscientious	Considerate	Co-ordinator
Creative	Creator	Customer-focused	Decisive
Dedicated	Dependable	Designer	Determined
Developer	Diplomatic	Discreet	Editor
Efficient	Encourager	Energetic	Enthusiastic
Even-tempered	Facilitator	Flair	Flexible
Forceful	Forecaster	Friendly	Genuine
Gregarious	Honest	Humorous	Imaginative
Implementer	Independent	Influencer	Initiator
Innovative	Integrator	Interpreter	Inventive
Inventor	Knowledgeable	Leader	Logical
Loyal	Manager	Mediator	Modest
Monitor	Motivator	Motivator	Optimistic
Organiser	Organised	Originator	Patient
Perceptive	Perfectionist	Persistent	Persuasive
Positive	Practical	Presenter	Quick-thinking
Realistic	Reconciler	Relationships	Reliable
Researcher	Resourceful	Responsible	Reviewer
Scientific	Self-reliant	Sensible	Sincere
Solver	Supportive	Systematic	Tactful
Thoughtful	Tidy	Tolerant	Understanding
Unselfish	Versatile	Visionary	Witty

Panning for gold – summarising exercises 1 and 2

First, reduce the number of words you have selected to between, say, six to eight. Then reduce them further to your top three. In the following example, the co-author had a shortlist of seven words. Of these three words, "create", "build" and "enable" stood out.

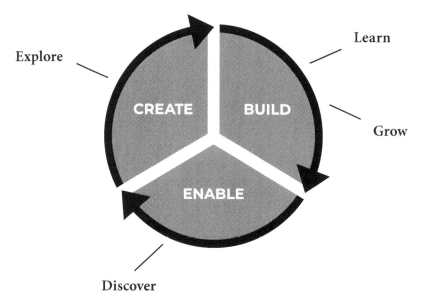

Now think about your top learned behaviours:

1. List your main knowledge and learned behaviours that you want to incorporate in your CV and mention at interviews.
2. What learned behaviours do you want to use less of or stop using? (eg you are fed up with doing budgets!)

Summary

Well done for diligently working through this chapter. The information you have gathered will help point you towards the type of jobs you would enjoy and excel in.

We suggest that you keep a note of your top three talents and strengths in a place where you can see them each day. You should weave them into the personal statement of your CV (Chapter 7).

You should also introduce them when networking (Chapter 6) and during interviews (Chapter 8). Potential employers are interested primarily in what you have achieved. In Chapter 6, we explain how you can communicate your achievements using a STAR format.

Useful resources

Book
◆ Chapters 2 and 3 of *Creating a Purposeful Life* by Richard Fox, especially for your top three unique talents and strengths.

Websites
◆ https://www.16personalities.com/free-personality-test – Discover your personality type and how that can help you unlock your potential.
◆ https://www.strengthscope.com/ – Its mission is "to reveal the unique strengths of people across the world enabling them to bring their most authentic and inspired selves to work and to life every day".
◆ https://www.viacharacter.org/ – This free self-assessment takes less than 15 minutes and provides a wealth of information to help you understand your best qualities.
◆ https://www.gallup.com/cliftonstrengths/en/home.aspx – This seeks to explain how you are uniquely powerful.

Chapter 3

Be guided by what you truly value

"Let what you truly value guide you – or be driven by the hustle and bustle of life, the demands of others and the vagaries of circumstance. The choice is yours."

—Anon

Learning outcomes

By the end of this chapter you will have:

◆ identified your own most important values and how to meet them

◆ established a set of goals for your life and for your job search.

Why do values matter?

Values have a direct effect on our behaviour: the way we live our lives and whether we feel satisfied or fulfilled. Our values influence our decision-making, risk-taking, goal-setting and how we spend our time, energy and money.

When we talk about values, we are not talking about things we think we "should" do or "should" like. Instead, we are talking about things that you, and you alone, personally value because you need them in order to be happy.

When you are job hunting, knowing your values is important:

◆ to determine what kind of work and organisation will bring satisfaction and fulfilment, especially if you are seeking a career change
◆ to recognise whether you are spending your time and resources most effectively to achieve your goals.

Values might encompass:

◆ something you care for or feel strongly about
◆ ideas and beliefs that really matter to you
◆ hidden factors that direct your dreams, ambitions and goals
◆ internal motivators
◆ a feeling of fulfilment when values are satisfied
◆ a determination of what life means to you
◆ behavioural influences.

For example, wanting to have control over where you work is a value. You might also value a collaborative environment or the ability to be creative in your work. Values are key to our happiness at work (and in life!).

If, for example, you have a value on the freedom to work any-where you want, and your company expects you in the office every day for 40 hours a week, you'll probably slowly become miserable.

Or, if you love having autonomy in your work and your organisa-tion believes in micromanagement, you'll probably be really unhappy.

Values are interesting, because when they are out of alignment in your place of work, then you are likely to feel it. You'll feel off, unhappy or misaligned, and you sometimes can't quite put your finger on why.

Identifying someone whom you consider to be a hero/heroine, and why, will help you start recognising the things that are important to you, what you value and what motivates you.

What motivates you?

When you know your motivators, you can make better decisions, meet deadlines, suffer less stress and engage more effectively.

We all have unique motivators and different strategies work for different people. For example, if you are motivated primarily when working closely with team members, you are unlikely to be happy as a research assistant working alone. Some people may be the complete opposite and thrive in a quiet, focused environment.

Unique gifts, talents and key capabilities

We are all unique. The way we filter all the information we receive differs from one person to another. As Stephen Covey, author of *The 7 Habits of Highly Effective People*, says: "We see the world not as it is, but as we are – or, as we have been conditioned to see it."

More importantly, each one of us has a unique story to tell based on the knowledge and experience we have acquired.

You are only on this planet once. So, why not spend some time unearthing your unique talents, gifts and strengths, identifying the unique contribution you could make to society and in your work?

EXERCISES

Exercise 1 – Who are my heroes/heroines?

◆ Identify one or two people you consider to be your "hero(es)/heroine(s)"– someone you admire for some reason. It may be someone you know, someone famous, someone from history, etc.

◆ Write down: What qualities or values do you admire?

◆ Do you recognise those values or qualities as being important to you in your own life?

Exercise 2 – What are my values?

Our values inform the way we operate our lives on a daily basis.

Review the following list of values and qualities, or characteristics we might value, and identify those words that jump out at you or that give you a strong gut reaction as being important to you.

Acceptance	Change	Creativity	Enthusiasm
Accomplishment	Charity	Cultural diversity	Excellence
Accuracy	Collaboration	Curiosity	Excitement
Achievement	Comfort	Decisiveness	Experimentation
Adventure	Communicativeness	Dedication	Expertise
Ambition	Community	Democracy	Fairness
Art	Compassion	Devotion	Fame
Attractiveness	Competition	Dignity	Family
Awareness	Concentration	Discovery	Feminism
Autonomy	Connectedness	Education	Financial security
Beauty	Contact with people	Encouragement	Flexibility
Calmness	Cooperation	Elegance	Forgiveness
Challenge	Courage	Empathy	Freedom

Freedom of choice	Knowledge	Pleasure	Status
Friendship	Laughter	Positivity	Support
Fulfilment	Leadership	Power and authority	Success
Fun	Learning	Pragmatism	Taking responsibility
Generosity	Leisure	Problem-solving	
Global awareness	Literature	Professionalism	The big picture
Global peace	Liveliness	Quality of Life	Thinking time
Grace	Living your dreams	Quiet	Thoroughness
Growth	Logic	Recognition	Tolerance
Guidance	Love – for myself	Reliability	Trust
Happiness	Love – for others	Respect	Understanding
Harmony	Making a difference	Responsibility	Uniqueness
Having a voice	Mastery	Results	Variety
Having dreams	Moderation	Risk-taking	Versatility
Health	Motivation	Routine	Vision
Helpfulness	Music	Security	Vitality
Honesty	Nature	Self-control	Vocation/purpose
Humour	Openness	Self-reliance	Wisdom
Imagination	Optimism	Sensitivity	Zest
Independence	Order	Sensuality	*Add any other values which are important to you that are not on this list.*
Influence	Originality	Service	
Innovativeness	Passion	Sharing	
Inspiring others	Patriotism	Simplicity	
Integrity	Peace	Sociability	
Intelligence	Persistence	Solitude	
Joy	Personal growth	Spirituality	
Justice	Physical challenge	Spontaneity	
Kindness	Play	Stability	

Using the table below, create a list of your 20 most important values, without trying to put them in any order. This should be a "gut reaction" so it need not take lots of time to complete.

My Top 20 Values

Now, edit the list down to your six most important values. To help identify the order of priority, it may help to ask yourself: Which of these values is truly the most important to me in life? If only one could be satisfied, which would it be? This is the number one value. Move down the list asking which remaining value is the next most important, and so on.

My six most important values

Reflection

Invite a friend or coach to discuss with you why you have chosen these particular values and what each one means to you. Have them ask you what the values really mean to you and challenge you as necessary. Make a note of the responses for future reference, and put them in order of priority.

1.

2.

3.

4.

5.

6.

Sorting my values

Looking at your six most important values, which are expressed in your current/most recent job and in your outside work/social life? Reflect on all areas of your work and life such as people, working conditions, what you love to do, your goal or purpose in life, your knowledge, level of responsibility/salary and your preferred geographical location.

	These values ARE expressed	These values are NOT expressed
WORK – most recent or previous jobs		
OUTSIDE WORK – leisure, hobbies, relationships, etc		

How can I bring my most important values into my life?

Write down or discuss with a friend or coach ways that you can bring your values into different aspects of your life. If your chosen field of work cannot meet all your values, how can you ensure that they are met in other areas of your life?

1.

2.

3.

4.

5.

6.

Exercise 3 – What motivates and inspires me?

Action precedes momentum and it is easy to get overwhelmed by all you have to do in order to find fulfilling work and change careers.

Ask yourself: "What are the three most important things I can do to help my career right now? And of those three, which will make the biggest impact?"

Make a note of these three in priority order. Keep that list somewhere accessible and review it every week.

It is also useful to identify how you respond to expectations, which can help you put in place strategies to make it more likely that you will achieve your aims.

Useful resources

Books

♦ *Creating a Purposeful Life* by Richard Fox; Infinite Ideas Limited

♦ *Get the Life You Love and Live It* by Arvind Devalia, Nirvana Publishing.

Websites

- http://www.stevepavlina.com/articles/living-your-values-1. htm – aims to help you further with identifying and living your values.
- https://quiz.gretchenrubin.com/four-tendencies-quiz/ – helps you identify your personal motivation tendency.

Chapter 4

Personal barriers and self-limiting beliefs

"The day came when the risk to remain tight as a bud was more painful than the risk it took to blossom."

—Anais Nin

Learning outcomes

By the end of this chapter you will:

- ◆ understand what personal barriers may be hindering your job search
- ◆ have strategies for overcoming your personal barriers.

Why this is important

To find your dream job, you have to believe you can do it.

Lack of response to applications, not getting interviews or failing to get through to the next round can really knock self-confidence and self-esteem. Having confidence in yourself and your decisions moving forward is often one of the biggest indicators of success, so it is worth taking the time to complete these exercises.

"Barriers" may be internal or external, but you have a choice about how you perceive the situation. Personal barriers may include:

- lack of motivation
- lack of confidence
- cultural barriers – eg, what is acceptable/unacceptable type of work for men/women
- feeling inadequate
- being unqualified
- self-limiting beliefs.

Self-limiting beliefs

Self-limiting beliefs or assumptions are thoughts we hold that become obstacles to us moving in a particular direction, eg, someone in their 50s believing that they are too old to re-train for a new career.

Internal beliefs are those imposed on ourselves (I'm too old for this, I'm not clever enough to do that, etc.), while external beliefs are those imposed on us by others (you'll never be able to do that, that's not a job for women, etc.).

You may have one or more self-limiting beliefs that need to be challenged and changed; otherwise, they will continue to get in your way and become self-fulfilling prophesies.

Common examples of self-limiting beliefs are:

- "I'm over 50 and no one will want to employ me."
- "I have been in the x sector for 20 years and I have left it too late to switch to another sector."
- "I have a disability so I would be eliminated at the first hurdle."
- "I don't have any contacts."

None of the above is true.

Some Beliefs and Assumptions Can Become Self-Fulfilling

... and because they are close to the core of who we are, we look for evidence to prove them to ourselves.

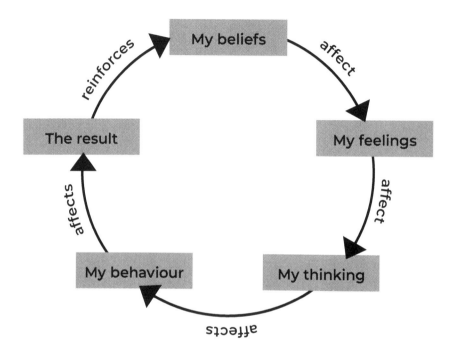

Changing a Belief or Assumption

... can have a domino effect.

Change a belief and then we change our behaviours.

We can change beliefs if we want to. Prove this fact to yourself by thinking back to something you used to believe – but no longer do.

Some examples of "limiting" beliefs
Global beliefs – generalisations:

- If you trust people, they'll take advantage of you.
- If I even look at a cake, I put on weight.
- If you really loved me, you'd know what I need before I have to tell you.
- Life's a b**** and then you die.

Empowering beliefs:

- Most people go out of their way to help me. Isn't it great?
- I can really enjoy cake when I have it as an occasional treat.
- When I tell you what I need, you always respond positively. Aren't I lucky to be loved?
- Life is what you make of it – you get out what you put in.

Do you recognise any of these?

- I **must be** liked by everyone.
- Everything I do **must be** perfect.
- All the people I live or work with **must be** perfect.
- If things go wrong, it **must be** my fault.
- If I'm not happy, it **must be** someone else's fault.
- It's **always** better to avoid an argument than to raise a problem.
- Disagreement/conflict **must be** avoided at all costs.
- **People**, including me, do not change.
- **Everything** was better in the good old days.
- If I feel overworked, I **must be** incompetent.
- There is **only one way** of seeing any situation – "The true way".

- You **can't** teach an old dog new tricks.
- Change is **never** for the better.
- Change is **always** for the better.
- When I first meet people, they **always** think I'm boring.

Confidence and self-esteem

"Whether you think you can or think you can't, you're right."
—Henry Ford

Closely linked to your self-limiting beliefs is whether you believe:

- in yourself
- in how worthy and capable you are – self-confidence
- that you are worthy of respect from others – self-esteem.

Both your self-confidence and self-esteem can take a knock during your job search, which in turn can cause stress, anxiety, unhappiness, poor decision-making and under-achievement. Improving these qualities can dramatically affect the way you approach life, and at this particular time, your search for a new job.

The exercises in this chapter provide a framework for you to build self-confidence and self-esteem, so you can:

- view your circumstances as a challenge to overcome and an opportunity to embrace, enabling you to make changes more easily
- deal more easily with setbacks, with improved resilience and the desire to learn from situations
- have more faith in yourself, which will give others confidence in you.

An attitude of gratitude – changing your view of the world

"Gratitude unlocks the fullness of life. It turns what we have into enough, and more. It turns denial into acceptance, chaos to order, confusion to clarity. It can turn a meal into a feast, a house into a home, a stranger into a friend. Gratitude makes sense of our past, brings peace for today and creates a vision for tomorrow."

—Melody Beattie

Job searching can be difficult and you might be feeling negative. This breeds pessimism and anger, which can lead to depression. Gratitude helps to reframe situations in a positive context, looking at what is right and good in your life and seeing the good in yourself and others.

EXERCISES

Exercise 1 – Personal reflection on barriers/self-limiting beliefs

What are your main barriers/self-limiting beliefs? Write them down! Where did those barriers/beliefs come from? How keen are you to overcome them? What is the evidence for and against?

Decide what belief you want to change…

LIMITING BELIEF OR ASSUMPTION

. . . .

. . . .

. . . .

. . . .

. . . .

. . . .

EVIDENCE:

. . . .

. . . .

. . . .

. . . .

. . . .

. . . .

AN ALTERNATIVE BELIEF (based on fact)

. . . .

. . . .

. . . .

. . . .

. . . .

. . . .

Imagine another person with this alternative belief.
What sorts of things would they feel? What would they
do or say?

. . . .

. . . .

. . . .

. . . .

. . . .

. . . .

. . . .

. . . .

. . . .

Can you do or say these things? When will you practice?

. . . .

. . . .

. . . .

. . . .

. . . .

. . . .

. . . .

. . . .

. . . .

Exercise 2 – Self-confidence

Think about your general level of self-confidence at the moment and rate it on a scale of 1-10.

Work through the following six steps:

1. In which situations do I feel self-confident? Can be work, leisure, etc.

2. What am I like when I am full of self-confidence? E.g., "I can do..." "I can be..."

3. In which situations do I lack self-confidence?

4. What am I like when I have low self-confidence?

5. Recognise that self-confidence is **WITHIN ME** for 1 and 2.

6. How can I retrieve it and add to it for 3?

Going Deeper

Now write a sentence stating your intention; for example, "My topic is my work and I'd like to find a career I really love."

My topic is . . . . and I'd like to . . . .

. . . .

On a scale of 1 to 10, where are you with this goal currently?

. . . .

What is your critical voice telling you about this topic at the moment?

. . . .

Now go forward in your mind to a point in time when everything in this area is exactly as you'd like it, where you've reached 10 out of 10. What are you doing which shows you that this issue has been resolved?

. . . .

What do you see happening that shows you've achieved what you wanted?

. . . .

What are other people saying to you?

. . . .

What are you thinking and feeling now that this is resolved?

. . . .

What benefits have you experienced?

. . . .

What impact has this had on other areas of your life? How has it impacted your work, your relationships, your health, etc.?

. . . .

Now, imagine what you'd be thinking and feeling and doing if nothing had changed and you hadn't achieved this goal.

. . . .

What would your critical voice be saying?

. . . .

What would your wiser voice be saying?

. . . .

What would you be feeling?

. . . .

Now, list all the different elements of your goal – the things you'll need to achieve in order to reach that 10-out-of-10 place.

. . . .

Look at your list, connect with your wisest self, and ask: "What's the next right thing to do in this situation?" Which point from your list needs to be tackled first? If the first step is a tiny one, choose the next three things you need to do to move forward with this goal. Circle them.

Your critical voice may be interfering. That's fine. Write down what it says, then counter what it says with some of the wisdom you've found.

At this point, you should have one to three action points you could potentially take towards your goal.

How would you rate your levels of self-confidence now on a scale of 1-10?

Just thinking about times when you are self-confident and strategies for increasing confidence in other circumstances may have increased your score, proving that we can change our perception of ourselves and our mindset to the job at hand – your job search.

Exercise 3 – Start a gratitude journal

Every day this week write down five things you are grateful for. At the end of the week, look back and take stock of the little things that you have been thankful for throughout the week. Making a habit of this creates new neural pathways and can really change your outlook on life.

Useful resources

Books

- *Creating a Purposeful Life* by Richard Fox. See Chapter 4 on beliefs and values, Chapter 14 on how to overcome self-limiting beliefs and the appendix for two worked examples.
- *Why losing your job could be the best thing that ever happened to you* by Eleanor Tweddell, Penguin Random House UK

Website

- http://www.mindtools.com/pages/article/newTCS_84.htm – Quiz: how self-confident are you? The Mindtools website also contains useful tips on building self-confidence.

Chapter 5

Putting all the pieces together to find a job

"If you haven't found it yet, keep looking."

—Steve Jobs

Learning outcomes

By the end of this chapter you will:

- know your Unique Value Statement (UVS)
- have identified your top three job or career options
- understand the key elements in job adverts.

Why this is important

It's time to take all of the work you've done so far – your perfectly written novel; your unique talents and strengths; your values; and what motivates and inspires you – and analyse them. Start to consider:

◆ What trends are you seeing?

◆ Which one or two things stand out?

This will help you to begin to brainstorm the job or career that will work for you.

Your Unique Value Statement

To help narrow down your options, you can create your Unique Value Statement (UVS). This will be the guiding light for your brainstorming process – your North Star.

There is probably a theme in your answers. For example, if you like both helping people and are interested in interior design, your UVS may be to help others by designing their homes.

One of our clients included the words "creativity" in 75% of her answers and "recognition" in about 50%. Two big themes. Is it any wonder that her UVS involves connecting her art to local galleries? Use your theme as a guide for helping you find that broad statement.

Bear in mind your greater purpose will be about you but also express how you serve the world.

For example: Joanna's (*the co-author's*) UVS isn't just to be happy in her career; it's to help others find a fulfilling career. Ultimately, your UVS is about where you fit in the world, and what you have to offer. Your job within this chapter is to look at the trends and themes you see and begin to put them together in one broad statement. This may not be easy but Exercise 1 will help.

Studying job adverts

Once you are clear on your unique talents, strengths and what you truly value, it is time to study job adverts. But remember, this is just one small part of the search process. Fewer than 30% of jobs are advertised and the following chapters will take you through some of the other ways to seek work.

When you read the advert, really try to understand the role – are you clear about its purpose and how it fits with the work of the organisation? It's difficult to do a great application if you don't understand these elements. Ask yourself: "What would I be doing in this job and why?" Aim to get better understanding of the employer's key needs.

Don't be put off if you can't do everything the advert is asking for. If you can do the majority it's worth considering applying. If you are not sure, ask the organisation or recruitment consultant.

What evidence can you give for the skills they are looking for? You may be able to give evidence of transferable skills. We will go through a STAR format to help you to demonstrate your ability and experience in Chapter 6.

Analyse the words used in the advert – what do they tell you about the person who will be a good fit for the organisation? Do they use the words "fast growing", "dynamic", "results orientated", "challenging"? Does this sound like the sort of organisation where you want to work?

Don't be put off by the job title – it may not be the same as a job you have done before or are seeking, but there are ways you can decide if it's a good fit for you. What are the responsibilities? Does it excite you? What qualifications are they asking for? What are the skills required?

Reading the job advert properly will give you lots of information to decide if this is the right job for you and how to make the best application you can.

EXERCISES

Exercise 1 – Unique Value Statement

Take your answers from all the exercises so far and start to analyse them. We want you to notice a few things:

1. What are the trends you are seeing?

2. Which one or two things stick out for you?

Set a timer for 20 minutes, turn off all distractions, and answer this question:

"What is my purpose in life?"

This exercise is important. As you write, you'll start off with your pre-recorded ideas and thoughts – things that are on the surface of your mind, often coming from your limiting beliefs. As you keep writing, you'll hit a deeper level of discovery, and you'll begin to peel back that top layer and write down things that are more rooted in your subconscious.

This may not be easy but keep writing. If you get stuck, take a break, but be sure to come back to this exercise later.

Take all the work you've done so far and condense it into a broad statement, eg:

- "My Unique Value Statement is to design homes to help people live in beautiful spaces."
- "My UVS is to help others find fulfilling careers."
- "My UVS is to help children thrive."

Keep it short and clear. You can then use what you've written as your North Star for your job or career brainstorming session.

Exercise 2 – Brainstorming the job or career for you

Your Unique Value Statement is the starting point for your brainstorming session. The rules of brainstorming are simple: there are no bad ideas. Take away any judgement and get ready to explore.

So, taking a look at your UVS, what jobs come to mind?

For instance, if we take Joanna's UVS, which is to help others find fulfilling careers, we can brainstorm a few different jobs.

UVS: help people find fulfilling careers so they live the life they want to live.

Jobs that fit this UVS:
1. Career counsellor
2. School careers adviser
3. Author/researcher on happiness and work (academic)
4. Writer/blogger (freelance)
5. Career coach
6. HR/outplacement specialist
7. Job centre adviser
8. Executive coach for organisations
9. Counsellor
10. Working for the military in a job placement service.

You can see that there are quite a few options, and we're just getting started. Now it's your turn to come up with 10 ideas and brainstorm them:

1. Jobs you can do as your own business or freelance.

2. Jobs you do for others as an employee working for an organisation.

3. Jobs that are in your current field but maybe with a different focus to what you do now or have done recently.

Next, rank your job ideas, with those you are most excited about at the top – 1, 2 and 3. What are 8, 9, and 10 – the ones that interest you least? Be aware you will have some judgements and ideas about yourself that are fuelled by your inner critic and limiting beliefs. Go with what excites you rather than what you think you "should" or "can" do.

Take a look at your list and circle your top three ideas – those are where you are going to start.

If you are feeling a little stuck, that's normal. Take your time, revisit your perfectly written novel, your unique talents and strengths, your values, what motivates and inspires you – and any themes that have arisen.

There is something out there that you can do well; and others will benefit from you doing it. Take your time, keep a notebook with you and write down the ideas as they come. Notice what you are curious about and start exploring that further.

You don't have to be sure about something to get an indication that you are on the right path – certainty comes later, after you have explored options and seen what motivates you, versus what slows you down.

It's now time to start investigating these ideas and see where they lead you. Google them, read about them, connect with those on social media who do those roles, set up some calls with people to learn about them. Real conversations matter because they can give you information you can't get anywhere else. Talk to several people in any one field. You want to have an informed view of each potential career.

Volunteering may help you learn new skills and gain some experience for your CV. Do an internet search or ask people you know and your social media connections if they know of any opportunities.

Exercise 3 – Studying job adverts

Review the sample job advert and points below.

Now find a job advert and use the internal research you have done to see if the role matches with what you offer, need and want.

Job title: Research Executive ◄──────── Don't dismiss a role by the job title – many skills are transferable.

Company: The Marketing Corporation, London

Salary: Competitive

We are offering a great opportunity to join a rapidly growing marketing consultancy as a research executive. You will join a small team with responsibility for project managing client market research projects as well as gathering high quality market intelligence on issues, news and trends.

Do your research – how long has the company been established, how quickly are they growing, how many people do they currently employ? What kind of clients do they work for? Think about how well you would fit in. Does the work sound interesting, would you be using skills that you enjoy using?

We regularly publish reports, papers and opinion articles that are widely read by the industry and commented on by both trade and national press. A key part of this role is to support the research for these publications, and where appropriate take ownership of writing and promoting them. You will be required to build up strong contacts in the media to ensure the effective promotion of articles to reach the widest possible audience.

We strive to attract the best talent, to provide the best career development opportunities and provide relevant training.

Make sure your CV and letter covers all the points here. Think about what you've done throughout your qualifications, work experience, volunteer experience and life experience, and where you can get evidence of skills they want. Because the job asks for exceptional attention to detail, you must make sure there are NO mistakes in your application.

Person requirements
- Degree level 2.1 minimum
- Experience of qualitative and quantitative data collection
- Strong research skills
- Excellent writing, editing and proofreading skills
- Exceptional attention to detail
- Competent user of MS Word and Excel

- Experience of preparing and delivering presentations
- Must be able to meet tight deadlines and handle multiple ongoing projects

Start date: As soon as possible

Apply with CV and letter by 5pm on Friday 25 February 2021. Interested applicants can ring Jo Cooper Ext 2445 to discuss the requirements of the position further.

Check the start date so you know if this is suitable for you.

Organisations often provide this kind of contact – it's a great idea to get in touch with a few relevant questions. It helps highlight your interest in the organisation and the role and it could help your application stand out as you may have additional information that other applicants don't have.

Useful resources

Book

◆ *Designing Your Life: How to Build a Well-Lived, Joyful Life* by Bill Burnett; Penguin Random House USA.

Website

◆ https://www.cvscan.uk – CVScan is an online job description keywords comparison tool with instant match results to optimise your CV, resumé, cover letters, or LinkedIn profile with keywords.

Chapter 6

The importance of networking for your career

"It's not what you know, it's who you know."

—Anon

Learning outcomes

By the end of this chapter you will:
- be able to develop your own personal contact map and record-keeping system
- feel confident in networking
- know some new ways to approach your job search.

What is networking?

Networking is about making connections. It is a two-way process – listening to what other people have to say and telling others about yourself. Think of it as a "drip-feed" of information that enables you to maintain relationships and keep your contacts informed.

It is crucial in the job hunt because at least 70% of jobs are gained through networking. This rises to as high as 85% for more senior jobs.

You need to be ready to connect people within your web who may be of interest to each other.

With a job search, you need to target your networking so that you use your time wisely.

Networks begin with a genuine interest in people and an enthusiasm for sharing information. We each have a personal web, which contains our connections of people, such as family, friends and social media connections. Every person you meet, in any aspect of your life, is part of your personal web. Networking when you are job hunting is simply a more focused form of what we all do in everyday life.

Optimise your LinkedIn pages, again stating the roles you are seeking and what you can offer a potential employer, backed up by your achievements. Join and take an active part in relevant LinkedIn groups, connect with other individuals and recruiters, thus adding value and demonstrating your expertise. Potential employers are likely to look at your social media pages, so if you are, for example, on Facebook remove any unhelpful photos.

A key tool in networking is to have a ready-made "elevator" speech, ie, one or two sentences that convey what you can offer. This statement is also useful in interviews when answering the question: "Can you tell me something about yourself?"

If you don't access these connections as part of your job search, you are missing out on a vital channel.

How to create STARs for networking, CVs and interviews

Many employers use competencies to screen candidates at both the application stage and the interview. By creating a catalogue of your own competencies, you will be able to construct your CV/LinkedIn profile/application and practice for interviews based on the competencies identified in the job advert and job description.

The STAR – **S**ituation, **T**ask, **A**ction, **R**esult – technique helps you highlight a past experience (**situation**), explain your **task**, highlight your solution (**action**) and explain the outcome (**result**). This allows the prospective employer to see evidence of your abilities and compare this with required competencies.

The six degrees of separation

The idea of "six degrees of separation" suggests that anyone on Earth can meet another in the world with a maximum of six mutual connections between them and the other person – be that through acquaintances, friends or members of their family.

This is a helpful way of looking at things, since networking is the most effective way to get a job. So consider your ideal job and who you might need to meet in order to get it. According to the six degrees of separation theory, it's doable.

With this theory, you can reach any person on the planet through no more than five intermediaries. For example, imagine that you want to meet the head of marketing of an IT company, and that, perhaps, you have a relative who works in a marketing agency.

She doesn't know that person, but she once lived in London with someone who worked in IT. And they, in turn, know someone who sometimes does temporary work in the company you are interested in. And they, in turn know the receptionist. And they, in turn, know the marketing assistant, who works for the head of marketing. It may sound convoluted, but it's surprising how easy it can be to make contact with the person you want to meet if you think creatively.

Networking is about building and valuing contacts, relationships and personal connections with people around you – not just when you are looking for work but all the time. As well as face to face, social media platforms such as LinkedIn and Facebook can play their part.

Networking is a valuable skill and worth being aware of in all aspects of your life. It's as much about being there for others, showing you care about them as human beings and offering them help, as it is about as seeking something for yourself. It can start with simply saying hello as you pass them in the corridor or street.

Using networking as part of our job search

Networking is an effective pathway towards getting a job. It is about expanding your connections, opening up avenues to new information and meeting new people. As we have learned, over 70% of jobs are not advertised and recruitment takes place in other, more informal ways. In particular, small businesses virtually never advertise. They recruit new employees by many other means, usually through some form of networking and word of mouth.

By spending time on increasing your networks, you enhance your opportunities for hearing about a job by a means other than answering a job advert. Set aside time each week to dedicate to this activity.

Remember that networking is a two-way street. This makes it feel less exploitative for those worried about making contacts just to tap them for information. The process has been described as a "chain of helpfulness". It's not just about asking "What can you do for me", but first of all thinking "What/who do I know who might help you?"

LinkedIn now offers employers a recruiter licence so that in just a few keyword searches recruiters and employers can easily compile a list of their ideal candidates and approach them.

Either the candidate is being approached directly by the employer, or the candidate is proactively getting in front of the employer and accessing the hidden job market.

You can also set up job alerts on sites such as LinkedIn, Guardian

Jobs and Simply Hired. You may wish to research specific organisations and industries by researching professional associations, industry journals, or specialty sites related to your area of interest.

The Elevator Pitch

The job search Elevator Pitch is a bit like the profile at the beginning of a CV. It is a clear, concise message that can be delivered in the time it takes an elevator to travel from one floor to the next – telling someone exactly who you are and what opportunities you are looking for. Ideally, it is no longer than two sentences.

The Elevator Pitch can be used in many ways, including:

◆ the casual networking opportunities we encounter every day – at the school gates, sitting next to someone on a train, in the doctor's waiting room, etc

◆ events designed specifically for networking (where your pitch may be as short as 15-30 seconds)

◆ career or job fairs

◆ cold calls to employers, including leaving a voicemail message

◆ job interviews, where the Elevator Pitch can provide the answer to at least two common interview questions: "Tell me about yourself" and "Why should I recruit you?" You can back up your pitch with examples of relevant achievements using the STAR format.

Using professional networking sites and social media

You will be aware of the many professional networking sites and social media sites, such as LinkedIn, Facebook and Twitter. You probably have accounts on one or more. If you don't access these as part of your job search, you are missing out on an important channel of networking – both for you finding out about jobs and for recruiters finding out about you.

LinkedIn is the most important site to use.

Most executives and managers, if approached directly on LinkedIn, would agree to a call or meeting when contacted by a legitimate, well-qualified person to discuss their interest in joining the business. Be creative, consider sending a voice note on LinkedIn (people are more likely to respond to a voice note than an email) or post a letter.

This is a highly underused way of accessing the hidden job market to get in front of employers before they know they need you.

EXERCISES

Exercise 1 – Analysing your achievements

Many employers use competencies to screen candidates at both the application stage and the interview. By creating a catalogue of your competencies, you will be able to construct your CV/LinkedIn profile/application and practice for interviews based on the competencies identified in the job advert and job description.

The STAR technique helps you use past experiences/**s**ituations, your **t**ask, your **a**ctions/solutions and the **r**esult/outcome to help the prospective employer see evidence of your abilities and compare this with required competencies.

Situation
Task
Action
Result

- Prepare and analyse a set of achievements to show knowledge, skills, and strengths and be prepared to describe them using STAR.
- Study an advert for a job you are interested in and whatever information you have about the job/company to identify the likely core competencies, eg, working in a team, customer focus, etc. Identify STARs for each of these competencies so that you have evidence of them.
- Prepare your stories and practice some competency questions for interviews.
- Keep the description of the situation and task brief and provide more information about what you did, what strengths and skills you used and what the outcome was.

	Core competency	Situation	Task	Actions and strengths	Result
1					
2					

	Core competency	Situation	Task	Actions and strengths	Result
3					
4					
5					
6					

Exercise 2 – My personal contact map

The first step is to list your adult family members, neighbours, friends/others you know socially, ex-colleagues and all other business contacts.

When you are relatively clear on the two or three types of jobs you would like to pursue, contact each person, asking them who they could introduce you to so that you can learn more about a particular industry/sector. This new contact may, in turn, introduce you to a friend of theirs who has a job vacancy.

You must also be ready to connect people within your web who you can help as well.

In his book "How To Get a Job You'll Love", John Lees talks about the difference between numbers and connections. "If four people are acquaintances, there are 12 one-to-one relationships between them. If you add one more person, you get 20 relationships. Six people means 30 connections, seven makes 42. As the personal web goes beyond 10, the number of possible interactions explodes."

With a job search, you need to target your networking so that you use your time wisely. Record the things you have in common, the things that are important to them (like the names of their family members), where you met or who introduced you and any useful nuggets of information or contacts that they provided. Also remember to ask: "What can I do for you?"

Complete the personal contact map below with areas of your life such as neighbours, ex-colleagues, friends/others you know socially, family, social media contacts, etc. Expand on each area to consider all of the networking possibilities.

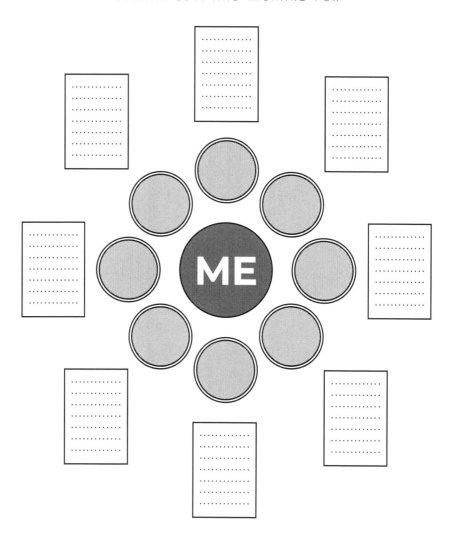

Exercise 3 – The six degrees of separation

Consider the six degrees of separation mentioned earlier:

- ◆ Who knows who?
- ◆ Who do I contact, and how?

Think of one person you would like to meet. Write down or discuss with a friend or professional coach how you could bring about that meeting, thinking about each person's contacts and connections. You may have to start at the end and work backwards, or start with your own connections and work forwards.

When you think about people you want to meet, imagine crossing a giant net in which each knot in the mesh is a contact who leads you to the next contact. In this way, you reach your goals one step (or contact) at a time.

Exercise 4 – Speculative letters or emails

When a speculative letter or email hits the manager's desk or inbox right at the time when s/he needs to employ someone, you are likely to at least get invited for a conversation – and you may be the only person the company interviews if you meet the employer's needs. LinkedIn provides a golden opportunity to contact hiring managers directly.

A speculative letter or email should contain three paragraphs:

1. "You need…" – based on your research, you make some comment about their business which suggests that you know a little bit about them, eg, "I read with interest that you are looking to expand…"

2. "I have…" – a brief summary of what you can offer them, including one or two points which demonstrate how you might be able to meet their needs, eg, "I have 10 years' experience in book-keeping, including preparing draft annual accounts and VAT returns, and am willing to do part-time or full-time, depending on your requirements."

3. "Let's meet…" – make a positive statement inviting them to contact you, or telling them you will follow up, eg, "I would welcome the opportunity to meet with you to discuss any opportunities that might arise from this. Please feel free to contact me; [*or preferably*] I am happy to call you next week to introduce myself."

Attach a copy of your CV to the letter or email so the recipients can see what you have to offer.

Exercise 5 – The Elevator Pitch

The Elevator Pitch is one to two sentences which tell people who you are and exactly what you are looking for. It can be used in so many ways, including networking and interviews.

Draw up your Elevator Pitch (based on suggestions from the business school at Pepperdine University, California):

1. Who am I?
2. What do I offer?
3. What problem is solved?
4. What are the main contributions I can make?
5. What should the listener do as a result of hearing this?

For example:

> "Hi, I'm Katie Clarke. I develop mobile applications that businesses use to train their staff remotely. This means that senior managers can spend time on other important tasks. I'm unique because I prioritise finding out exactly what the client and end-user need. This means that, on average, 95 per cent of our clients are happy with the first version of their app. I would love to hear more about how you train new staff members."

Exercise 6 – How to be found on LinkedIn

Chapter 7 covers how to create an optimal LinkedIn profile so you may wish to ensure you have an optimised profile before starting this step.

- **Adjust your settings**

  In your profile settings ensure your profile highlights that you are 'Looking for job opportunities'. You can choose whether all LinkedIn members or only recruiters can see that you're open to job opportunities.

- **Build your network to 500+ connections**

  The more connections you have, the more visible you will be when recruiters and hiring managers search for candidates. If a recruiter searches and you are not in their top three levels of connections, you may not show up. Use the advanced people search function to find key contacts in your market. Reach out and add them to your network with a personalised request letting them know why you are interested in networking with them. Even if they don't have any job leads, becoming connected to them will help expand your network and increase your visibility. Some key contacts to reach out to are recruiters who work for your target companies, recruiters representing local staffing agencies/firms, hiring managers and others with a background similar to yours. Many recruiters and employers advertise solely via a post on LinkedIn rather than paying to advertise the vacancy on the job boards so building your connections is incredibly important.

- **Engage**

  Comment and like other people's posts sharing your expertise or beliefs. What can you put back into the ecosystem? Build relationships, show support and start to build your personal brand.

◆ **Create**

Creating content is how you can take this to the next level and position yourself as an expert in your field. What are the top three things you know more about than 90% of other people? What three values do you want to get across (how do you want to make people feel)? What are the top three things your audience want? You can write articles, create short posts, share industry insights, or share what role you are seeking next.

◆ **Join groups**

You can, and should, join many groups, as this will instantly increase your visibility. Relevant groups include those related to your university, previous employers and industry/skills/job title, associations, as well as local networking groups.

◆ **Use keywords**

One of the most important factors in getting found is keyword optimisation. What keywords are recruiters searching for to find you? Pick your top five to 10 words and search your profile to find out how many times those keywords appear. They should be in your profile at least 10 times – and more for the most important or main keywords. Use both single words and phrases and think creatively about what words you would search for if you were in the recruiter's shoes.

◆ **Connect with both head and heart**

Even with the emphasis on keywords, your LinkedIn profile must be reader-friendly. Recruiters spend an average of six seconds looking at your profile, so make it interesting. Make it easy for others to find the relevant information.

Useful resources

Book

◆ *How to Get a Job You Love* by John Lees; McGraw-Hill Education

Websites

◆ https://www.thebalancecareers.com/how-to-use-networking-to-find-a-job-2058686 – how to use networking to find a job
◆ https://www.thebalancecareers.com/elevator-speech-examples-and-writing-tips-2061976 – for a further tutorial on preparing your own Elevator Pitch.

Chapter 7

Writing and improving your LinkedIn profile, CV/online applications and covering letters

"Your resumé says a lot about you. It determines whether you will be called in for an interview or not."

—Anon

Learning outcomes

By the end of this chapter you will:

◆ know some tools and tips to understand the purpose of the various online profiles and application stages of getting a job
◆ be able to develop your best LinkedIn profile, CV/online applications, portfolio and covering letters.

Updating my LinkedIn profile

Your LinkedIn profile is key in the current job market. It will get viewed much more often than your CV because it is available in the public domain. It can easily be found by recruiters, using keyword searches for those attributes requested by the employer. The exercise in this chapter will take you through the steps to get LinkedIn-ready.

Your LinkedIn profile is the shop window that may lead to somebody requesting your CV/online application. This leads to stage two – your CV/application, which has the aim of getting you an interview. It doesn't get you the job – that's the purpose of the interview.

Ninety-four percent of recruiters are active on LinkedIn, but only 36% of job seekers are. This gives you an incredible advantage to stand out and be found by companies seeking talent.

The exercises in this chapter will help you update your LinkedIn profile and use the platform to network effectively.

Which type of CV should I choose?

The CV/online application needs to demonstrate to the recruiter that you have the skills they are looking for and secure you an interview. Congruency of message is needed between what you offer and what the employer is seeking. You need to capture the reader's attention in a matter of seconds to make sure your CV ends up in the "Yes" pile.

There are two main types of CVs:

◆ **Chronological (traditional) CV**
   You use this type of CV if you are looking for a similar job. Include your personal statement, key achievements and your employment history, with your most recent position first. Then move backwards, listing your previous roles. This is the most popular style of CV, as recruiters are familiar with it. It lets them scan the most relevant information first and is scannable by applicant tracking software used to filter job applications.

◆ **Skills-based (functional) CV**

Use this format if you are new to work, want to take up a different role in the same sector or move to a different sector. Again, with this CV, include your personal statement, followed by a STAR paragraph on each of the key skills the potential employer is seeking, for example team leader, business developer, commercial awareness. You must have a ready stock of STARS so you can quickly select and tailor the ones containing the skills that the employer is looking for. This is a good choice for career changers but is not as popular with recruiters and applicant tracking systems.

Two less used types of CV that should be chosen only under certain circumstances are:

◆ **Creative CV**

These are most suited to creative roles such as graphic design, media, marketing, and brand consulting. These types of jobs require highly skilled creative people. Therefore, a creative CV is a good choice to showcase your skills and past work.

◆ **Combination CV**

A combination CV is often a choice by people who want to make career change. To make a combination CV, you should first mention skills and expertise followed by educational qualifications and work experience. Writing a combination CV is tricky. It needs to grab the attention of employer from the beginning.

Exercise 2 will help you decide which one is relevant for you.

What to include and what to leave out

The recruiter who receives your CV is likely to run it through an applicant tracking system (ATS) and then still have dozens to sort through – and very little time to do so. Your CV will need to showcase your relevant experience, skills and qualities for that specific role in around six seconds. Simplification is the key to success.

A CV should comfortably fit on no more than two sides of paper.

Tailor your CV to the job advert and industry while communicating your uniqueness in your opening personal statement. The aim is to attract the head and heart of the recruiter when they first skim-read it.

In terms of the job description, highlight the adjectives that are used to describe the person; qualification, skills, and experience they're looking for; and include these in every section of your CV.

Tailor your skills to the specific job for which you are applying. Listing too many skills is overwhelming and you may lose the recruiter's attention.

Support your skills with practical examples of the impact they have had, backed up by facts and figures wherever possible.

Continuously ask yourself 'what's in it for them?'. They are not there to help you advance your career so reframe it 'to add real commercial value within…'.

Be ruthless with editing. This is not your life story.

CVs should include:

1. name, address, contact details, LinkedIn profile and website if relevant to the position you are applying for
2. a profile or personal statement
3. key achievements
4. standard headers like "Career History" and "Education"

5. job, employment or career history including month and year (don't leave any unexplained gaps) including:
    - responsibilities – short statements of the key parts of your job and the result
    - achievements – what you actually did and what you achieved
6. education/qualifications – highest qualification is usually the most relevant – language abilities, IT qualifications, certificates for other interests, etc.

They should not include:

- personal information such as date of birth, age, marital status and whether or not you have children
- current/last salary
- jobs that haven't lasted long and that you don't think are relevant
- school details/GCSEs, etc. unless you have just left school or college
- training courses that didn't result in a qualification
- photograph
- headers and footers, even for contact information, as applicant tracking systems often don't like them
- live links – while it is important to include your email address and LinkedIn URL on your CV, avoid live links (highlighted in blue), as some screening software will read those as a virus
- graphics, charts, graphs or tablets, unless you know that the applicant tracking system the company uses can handle these.

Proofread your CV. Incorrect spelling will land your CV in the bin.

Application forms/online applications/portfolios

Application forms are frequently used for recruitment in the public sector and are also becoming increasingly common in large companies. They provide a systematic way of comparing candidates, with all the required information presented in the same format. This is unlike CVs, which may vary in style, format and content and thereby make the initial screening process a lot slower.

Portfolios have traditionally been used by people in artistic professions as a visual way of illustrating their work and capabilities. However, a portfolio is increasingly being used by job seekers in other professions and industries, to stand out and go the extra mile.

There are some tips on completing applications/portfolios in the exercises of this chapter.

Covering letters to make a good first impression

A standard one-page covering letter is a courteous way of introducing yourself to the organisation and explaining which job vacancy you are applying for. It is usually the first contact you have with a potential employer, so it needs to make a good impression and include key elements. This is detailed in the exercises later in this chapter.

EXERCISES

Exercise 1 – Updating my LinkedIn profile

Here are some tips to work through when updating your LinkedIn profile:

- ◆ **Your photo**
  Adding a picture makes your profile 21 times more likely to be reviewed by others and nine times more likely to

receive connection requests. Use a photo showing you at your professional best and "interview-ready".

◆ **Top banner**

LinkedIn profiles with graphics have 11 times more chance of being viewed than those that don't. Use the wallpaper area to tell more of your story. What brings your role, experience and your personality to life? Search free image libraries like unsplash.com for inspiring pictures or use free software like canva.com to set your profile apart.

◆ **URL**

Change your personal URL to the linkedin.com/in/yourname format so that you can include your LinkedIn profile on your personal business cards, CV and professional correspondence.

◆ **Headline**

Use your job title, industry and relevant keywords for the job you are targeting. Make a list of what someone would search for when looking for you. Be sure to include your top two or three job titles and keywords in your headline. Edit via the mobile app to get more characters.

◆ **About**

This is an overview of how you define yourself professionally. What makes you different and stand out? What gives you an edge? Check out your industry peers and try to find your point of difference. Pepper your profile with keywords so you show up in searches. Add a call to action such as "I'd love to have a conversation. You can contact me by email/telephone."

Your "about" section should include the following:

- how many years of experience you have in a particular field or industry
- what you are passionate about
- what gets you excited enough to get out of bed each day and go to work
- how you have impacted your field/industry
- what significant contributions you have made for current/past employers
- what professional achievements you are most proud of.

◆ **Featured**

Showcase your best bits – work you are proud of, articles you have published, relevant industry articles or news you can link to.

◆ **Experience**

Make sure your experience is up to date, written in the past tense and tells the story of your growing skills. Emphasise your accomplishments and strengths, as you would on your CV. Focus on your target audience when you describe your background. Single out "what's in it for them", showcasing outcomes more than activities/ duties. Use keywords for the role you are targeting and a variety of word choices which can represent the same job. Complete as many of the sections as possible: experience, education, licences and certifications and volunteer experience.

◆ **Activity**

Actively engage. Get commenting, liking and sharing. Find people, pages or companies that align with your job search. Comment on their posts and share your views. This will keep you current and showcase your expertise.

◆ **Recommendations**

This is the most powerful part of your LinkedIn profile. Think about people who you have worked for or with. Start giving recommendations and don't be afraid to ask others for recommendations in return. This can make all the difference when recruiters and potential employers are looking at your profile.

◆ **Skills and endorsements**

Add your relevant skills and endorse others to encourage endorsements from those who build your credibility. The skills section is key for matching to job applications on LinkedIn and will determine whether you are a good fit for a role. Recruiters and hiring managers with premium or recruiter packages will get stats on profiles that are deemed to be good matches for the role, according to your keywords and skills. So, check which ones LinkedIn has chosen to show for you. Re-order so that the main skills you want to showcase are listed higher up.

◆ **Groups**

Be aware that the groups you join are listed on your profile, so they can either enhance or diminish your status. Join only those groups that help you to be seen in a positive light.

◆ **Managing your connections**

Adding connections helps expand your reach and allows you to come up higher in search results. Start by connecting to clients, prospective employers, recruiters, competitors, employees, associates and partners. LinkedIn allows you to sync your email address book with your LinkedIn account to connect to those you already know. Work on the understanding that while the individual might not be a suitable job search contact, someone in his/her network might be. Continually build your LinkedIn network by immediately connecting with every professional you come into contact with. Be proactive and reach out first. If there is a secret to job searching, this is it. Always follow up.

Exercise 2 – Which type of CV should I choose?

Consider the following:

◆ What are the most important qualities/skills for this position? Note the keywords and include these in your CV/ application.
◆ What problem/need could the organisation have? The organisation's website could prove useful as well as the job advert.
◆ What experience and skills do I have that can fulfil that need and solve that problem?

These questions will help you decide between the two main types of CVs:

◆ Chronological (traditional) CV – use this if you are looking for a similar job, as it starts with your most recent position first.
◆ Skills-based (functional) CV – use this if you want to take up a different role in the same sector or move to a different sector. It's a good choice for career changers but not as popular with recruiters and applicant tracking systems.

If you are a creative or are having a complete career change give thought to whether the two less common types of CV are relevant for you.

♦ Creative CV – these are most suited to creative roles such as graphic design, media, marketing and brand consulting. These types of jobs require highly skilled creative people. It is a good chance to showcase your skills and past work.

♦ Combination CV – this is often a choice by people who want to make career change. You should first mention skills and expertise followed by educational qualification and work experience. Writing a combination CV is a tricky job, and it is important that your CV grabs the attention of employer from the beginning.

Exercise 3 – CV top tips

Draw up your CV bearing in mind that the average recruiter looks at a CV for six seconds. Simplification is the key to success.

There are many ways to draw up a CV. You can find many free templates and CV builders online. Here are some tips to make your CV stand out from the rest.

♦ **Take your time**
The golden rule for job applications is to not rush. Give yourself ample time to collate the information for your CV and amend it for every single application. If you dash something off the night before a deadline and it leads to your application being discounted, all your experience and hard work will be wasted.

◆ **Structure your CV**

The most important information is a personal statement that lets the employer know who you are and most importantly what's in it for them. Keep this short and sweet – it should take up only one paragraph. Then ensure that your key achievements that are relevant for the role and industry are clearly laid out at the very beginning, as this is what will get you long-listed for an interview. Don't assume the recruiter will search through reams of information to find out if you're qualified for a position. They won't. Another great tip we have seen work is to include a quote from a reference right underneath your personal statement – this social proof and that someone will put their name to you will make your CV stand out from the crowd.

◆ **Keep it short**

While there's no hard and fast rule for the length of a CV, a couple of pages is usually regarded as the norm. Keep it punchy focusing on the result rather than the task, get your foot in the door and save the more involved explanations for your interview.

◆ **Keep it positive**

Your CV should not become a confessional, a list of mishaps or a series of excuses. Exorcise any references to failure – whether that's an examination, marital or business. Write positively and present your best face to the world, concentrating on the experience and achievements that have equipped you for a bright future. Bring language to life to make it a rich and dynamic reading experience. So for example instead of 'led' repeatedly you could use executed, chaired, coordinated, operated, planned.

◆ **Presentation**

Decorative patterns and eccentric formatting can often detract from your message and interfere with applicant tracking software which many organisations use to sift applications. Keep your CV uncluttered with short sentences, big margins around your text, and key points emphasised. Bullet points are useful and maximise the reader's ability to absorb information.

◆ **Tailor your CV**

A sure-fire way to boost your chances of getting an interview is to tweak your CV for each application you submit. Do your research on the business or organisation. What type of language do they use on their website to describe their staff and their outlook? Mirror this in your CV. Go through the job spec with a fine toothcomb, making sure to include examples proving relevant experience for all requirements of the role. Many recruiters use applicant tracking systems for the initial screening. To improve your chances of securing an interview, you need to include relevant keywords and match your competencies with those specified in the job advert. Every inch of your CV should be targeted to their needs. If you are talking about your hobbies consider what's in it for them, eg I am a *competitive* tennis player – if they are seeking a competitive individual for the role.

◆ **Avoid clichés**

Some words may have a detrimental effect on the impact of your CV. Recruiters see too many over-used clichés which say nothing about your skills or what you have achieved. Avoid phrases like "Excellent communication skills", "Strong team player" and "Results-oriented". Instead, talk about quantifiable achievements. Every point should be backed up with facts and figures – show not tell.

◆ **Don't be passive**

Be direct about what you have actually done rather than what you were responsible for. Action words written in the past tense add impact to your CV and better demonstrate what you've achieved and how you did it. They are more likely to catch the recruiter's attention. "Managed three direct reports" sounds much stronger and punchier than "Responsible for management of three direct reports".

◆ **Be honest**

Never embellish the truth in your job application, no matter how well you think you can cover it up. It takes only a quick phone call for the recruiter to discover that your First in Biochemistry from Oxford is actually an NVQ in Food Science from your local community college. Highlight the positives in your CV, but don't include blatant lies.

◆ **Don't leave unexplained gaps**

Recruiters will regard any unexplained gaps in your employment history with suspicion, so make sure to plug those holes. Times of unemployment can be adequately justified if you focus on the development of skills developed during that period.

◆ **Difficult scenarios**

If there were difficult experiences upon leaving your previous workplace, consider whether you would like to contact them to leave things on a good note. This may be difficult depending on your individual scenario but perhaps... 'I wish you all the best. Thank you for your time and the opportunity to date.'

It's a small world and you want to walk away knowing you did the best you could in that moment.

◆ **Education and qualifications**
Your work experience is usually more important than your qualifications unless you have only recently left school or college. Your highest qualification is usually the most relevant, so if you have a degree, you need not list your A-levels and GSCEs. Use this section to include other qualifications such as national vocational qualifications (NVQs) and language skills but omit references to any training courses that did not result in a qualification. They might make people question why you needed the training course.

◆ **References**
If you have room it is a nice touch to refer to two references including their contact details on your CV and consider inserting a quote from a reference. If someone is recommended, sales psychology means they are rated higher than someone who isn't.

◆ **Avoid photographs and personal information**
Unless specifically asked to provide a photo of yourself, leave it out. The skills, achievements and experience you describe – and not your hairstyle – should carry weight with the recruiter. In the same way, do not provide recruiters with information about your age, weight, height, religion, marital status or whether you have

children unless this is strictly relevant to your application. Salary details should be left out, as should interests or hobbies if they are neither relevant nor interesting.

◆ **Check, check, check... and then check again**
Any spelling or grammatical mistakes in your CV are going to create a negative perception in the mind of the recruiter. While spell-checkers can be useful, they don't catch everything and can often end up erroneously altering words to American spelling conventions. Get as many people as possible (who can spell) to go over your CV for typos and grammatical errors.

Exercise 4 – Using my STARs

During Chapter 6, we started to identify your skills and talents by looking at examples of what you did and achieved using the STAR format (Situation, Task, Action, Results). Now you can incorporate these into your CV in a way that tells a prospective employer what you did, how you did it – and, most importantly, the outcome or your contribution to the business. It gives a recruiter an indication of the skills you possess and how you use them to the benefit of the organisation.

Responsibilities and achievements

There is a big difference between what you were responsible for and what you actually did.

"Responsible for managing the quality management team."

This may tell someone what you did, but doesn't say whether you were good at it.

"Managed a team of five people who rolled out the new quality management initiative for the business, resulting in a 5 per cent reduction in manufacturing faults, worth £100,000 per year."

This tells someone more about what you did and, most importantly, what impact it had on the business.

Passive and assertive statements

Using strong action verbs in the past tense is an assertive way to describe your achievements. In contrast, passive statements say very little about who you are and what makes you different or unique. They leave the reader asking: "So what?"

"Introduced quality management and children's wear safety systems into new factories in Asia."

The above is talking about something you did, rather than an achievement. The recruiter may ask: "So what? What difference did it make to the organisation and what transferable skills do you have that would be useful for the job I am trying to fill?"

"Trained management teams in quality management and children's wear safety systems in six new factories in Asia, enabling the business to utilise new supply routes offering innovative product and cost savings while achieving the required standards."

This is a quantified achievement.

Business buzzwords

Recruiters are not keen on business buzzwords. Candidates often use phrases such as "excellent communicator", "strong team player" and "results-orientated", hoping to set themselves apart. However, these have become overused clichés which recruiters ignore. They are interested in your quantifiable achievements that demonstrate your skills.

Exercise 5 – Tips on completing application forms/ online applications

What kind of employer uses application forms and why?
Application forms are frequently used for recruitment in the public sector and are becoming increasingly common in large companies. They provide a systematic way of comparing candidates, with all the required information being presented in the same format, unlike with CVs which may vary in style, format, and content, making the initial screening process a lot slower.

Application forms may be used for a number of reasons:

♦ to ask specific questions about motivation, skills, attributes, or experience
♦ to ask for information not necessarily provided on a CV, for example, disclosure of criminal convictions
♦ if recruiting in batches, for example, for a graduate training programme
♦ To do an initial screening on writing skills, such as spelling, punctuation, and grammar.

If you have been asked to complete an application form, you are quite likely to be asked to submit a CV as well.

Top tips for completing job application forms

♦ Have all the information you need **before** you start filling out the application. Online applications are known to "time out" after a certain period, so do not risk losing the work you have done by spending time searching for dates, qualifications, etc. while you are mid-form.

◆ Be honest.

◆ Be accurate with your factual information and answer the questions with relevant examples to demonstrate your skills and achievements.

◆ Be legible, writing clearly and using black ink.

◆ Be concise.

◆ Avoid using jargon and abbreviations/acronyms.

◆ Use action words to start the sentences describing what you did, eg, Delivered… Instigated… Developed…, etc.

◆ Use one paragraph per example/idea and state the key information in the first sentence.

◆ Do not repeat yourself – use a different example for each question.

◆ Sign your application if you are asked to print it off and post or scan it to the recruiter.

◆ Complete all sections of the form. Do not leave anything blank.

◆ Proofread your application form, checking it for spelling and grammatical errors. If possible, print the form and check every section before hitting the "Submit" button or posting it.

◆ If possible, ask someone else to read through the form.

◆ Keep a copy of your application form to prepare for your interview.

Exercise 6 – The career portfolio

What is a portfolio?

A professional portfolio is an expanded form of a resumé or CV that demonstrates in more detail your skills and achievements and enables you to provide evidence to a prospective employer of your education, experience, unique strengths and talents, accomplishments, interests and professional goals and objectives.

It allows you to elaborate on the sections of your resumé you are most proud of, provide examples of your best work and include additional information about yourself relevant to the job you are applying for.

Who needs a portfolio?

Portfolios have traditionally been used by people in artistic professions as a visual way of illustrating their work and capabilities. However, job seekers in other professions and industries are increasingly using a portfolio as an additional tool in their armoury.

You can send a career portfolio in advance to an employer, along with your CV, to illustrate your skills and achievements in more detail. This may give you a higher chance of being invited to an interview.

Your portfolio can be used in job interviews to illustrate a point or demonstrate the breadth of your skills and experience. You can leave it with the interviewer as a strong reminder of who you are and what skills you bring to the role. It can also be helpful for school-leavers preparing a college or university application, for applying for scholarships or funding for training or sponsorship and for documenting your professional growth.

If you keep it up to date, it will be a useful tool throughout your career. Investing the time in creating a professional portfolio may be just what it takes to set you apart from the competition when applying for jobs. It will demonstrate your seriousness to potential employers and should improve your chances of being hired.

What should a portfolio contain?

A career portfolio will be personal and contain information relevant to the job you are seeking. If you plan to use a portfolio as a supporting document in an interview, as with your CV it is wise to tailor it to suit the company and role you are applying for.

What goes into your portfolio will vary depending on your industry or job role. You are using it to provide evidence of why the employer should recruit you. Therefore, ensure that the contents best demonstrate your skills, achievements, and future potential. You can include:

- **Resumé or CV** – A copy of your CV, including a summary of your education, achievements, and work experience, in whichever format suits your application.

- **Personal statement** – A description of who you are professionally. Include what is important to you and what you stand for, such as your work ethic, what motivates you, organisational interests, etc.

- **Professional goals** – A snapshot of where you see yourself in three to five years.

- **Career summary** – Items that demonstrate your career to date, as well as your work-related achievements, abilities, and skills, such as job descriptions from current and past employment

- **Work performance and letters of recommendation** – This may include awards, letters of appreciation, promotions and other recognition from previous employers, customers, colleagues, professors, etc, as well as job performance evaluations, satisfaction surveys from customers, students and patients, etc., and details of performance measures, such as sales volumes, health and safety records and cost control. All of this demonstrates how well you have achieved objectives and targets set by previous employers.

◆ **Skills and experience** – A more detailed demonstration of your core competencies, strengths and talents than your CV has space for. Try to include transferable skills and those relating to your area of expertise. For example:

- people skills such as team-working, leadership, negotiation and influencing
- communication skills covering written, verbal, and graphic communication, etc.

For each competency, include the name of the skill area; the performance or behaviour, knowledge or personal traits that contribute to your success; and your background and specific experiences of applying that skill.

◆ **List of achievements** – A detailed list of major accomplishments in your career to date, demonstrating what you have done in the past and indicating to a potential employer what you could do for them. Include examples of projects that you have managed or participated in, as well as examples of how you have resolved problems.

◆ **Samples of work** – This may include reports or papers you have written, examples of design work and projects, copies of presentations, etc. Choose the very best examples of your work and ensure these are relevant to the job for which you are applying.

◆ **Research, reports, articles and publications** – Include any published papers or articles that illustrate your written communication and language skills.

◆ **Education, training and continual professional development** – Include items that demonstrate your ability to learn and your desire for personal growth, such as diplomas, certificates and licences, awards, scholarships and other recognition, details of relevant training, workshops, seminars and conferences attended, vocational competitions entered/won, any professional associations of which you are a member, committees on which you have served and any other professional development activities.

◆ **Degrees, licences and certifications** – A description of any courses attended and degrees, licences and certifications held.

◆ **Volunteering/community service** – Describe your volunteer work and community service involvement, as well as pro bono work, especially where it relates to the job you are applying for or demonstrates your skills and strengths.

◆ **Referees** – Between three and five people who would be happy to vouch for your skills and abilities, achievements and experience. Ensure that you have sought permission from each referee, and include their full names, titles, contact details and relationship to you. At least one referee should be a former manager.

How should the portfolio be presented?

Job seekers might have an online portfolio, a paper portfolio or both.

Paper portfolios should be kept in a smart folder, binder or leather portfolio case. Choose the binder carefully, as the look of your portfolio will make an impression on the interviewer. The size and format may depend on the industry in which you work, or the type of role for which you are applying. Instead of a traditional portfolio of this kind, an online web-based portfolio or PDF may be more appropriate.

Ensure the contents are organised in a professional-looking, easy-to-access way. Include a table of contents, and if you're using a binder, separate the sections using labelled dividers. If you are creating a website for your portfolio, make sure it is easy to navigate.

Think about who will be looking at your portfolio and how much time s/he is likely to spend reviewing it. It is unlikely that anyone will have time to read long reports. Visual pieces will be easier to take in and will still provide a useful talking point. If someone is really interested in knowing more, you can offer to forward more detail to them later.

Develop one master portfolio with all your original documents. From this, you can pick and choose items to create different versions of your portfolio, tailored to fit the specific requirements of each employer. For each interview, produce a fresh portfolio, using copies of your most relevant documents. Present it in a folder that you are happy to leave with the interviewer should they request it.

The benefits of preparing a portfolio

By creating a professional portfolio, you will be preparing to make a strong impression on a prospective employer, as you will be spending time focusing on your skills and achievements.

As you think about what to include, you may need to contact former employers, managers or colleagues to help provide you with evidence of work you have completed, references, job descriptions, etc. Use the opportunity to let your contacts know that you are looking for a job.

Once you have created a portfolio, it is a good idea to keep it "alive", even after you start a new job. By updating your achievements on a regular basis, you are constantly reviewing the skills and experience you are building and will also be ready for any opportunity to demonstrate your skills in the future.

Exercise 7 – Covering letters top tips

Make a good first impression
A standard one-page covering letter is a courteous way of introducing yourself to the company and explaining which job vacancy you are applying for. It is usually the first contact you have with a potential employer, so it must make a good impression.

If you are applying by email, include your covering letter as an attachment rather than writing what you want to say into the email.

Customise your letter
Always write a targeted letter. If possible, find out the name and job title of the person to whom the letter should be sent, and address them by name, rather than Dear Sir/Madam.

What to include
The following format provides a guideline for what to include. In addition, an extra paragraph may be needed to explain any special circumstances, such as a career change.

- **Paragraph 1** – a positive, formal introduction making it clear why you are writing, indicating your interest in the job you are applying for and stating where you learned about the vacancy. You should also specify the documents you have enclosed (such as your CV or completed application form, etc).

- **Paragraph 2** – briefly explain why you are interested in the role and what attracts you to working with the organisation. This gives you the chance to demonstrate that you have done some research and that the role you are applying for fits with your career plans.
- **Paragraphs 3 and 4** – demonstrate your key skills and experiences with quantifiable evidence.
- **Paragraph 5** – end positively, indicating how you will follow up (typically with a phone call or an email) and telling them when you would be available for an interview.

Dear *[name of person sending to]*,

[Job Title]

I wish to apply for the role of *[job title]*. This role was brought to my attention by *[if possible, include a person or if not, then where you saw the role advertised]*. Please find enclosed my CV for your consideration.

As you can see from my attached CV, I have *[number]* years' experience working within the *[insert industry]*, and I believe the knowledge and skills built up during this time make me the right candidate for the role.

In my current role as a *[insert current role and organisation]*, I have been responsible for the *[key element of job applying for if possible]*, which, when coupled with my *[personal qualities they have specified]*, has helped the business to *[result]*.

I am confident that I can bring this level of success with me and help *[organisation]* build upon its reputation as *[insert reputation from website]*. With my previous experience and expertise, I believe my contribution will have an immediate impact on *[organisation]*.

Thank you for your time and consideration. I look forward to meeting with you to discuss my application further *[indicate how you will follow up/availability for interview etc]*.

Yours sincerely

[your name]

If you are emailing your CV and covering letter, type a short email, stating the position you are applying for and providing a list of attachments.

Useful resources

Books
◆ *CVs for Dummies, Cover Letters for Dummies* by Joyce Lain Kennedy; Wiley

Website
◆ https://www.livecareer.co.uk/ – CV and cover letter builders, professional writing services, interview tips, job listings and a convenient mobile app.

Many other useful websites provide a wealth of information and tips for writing CVs and covering letters as well as sample CVs and templates.

Chapter 8

Preparing for an interview

"If you think it's gonna be hard – it's gonna be hard."

—Kelly Trach

Learning outcomes

By the end of this chapter you will:

- have strategies in place for overcoming interview nerves
- know some top tips for interview success
- have knowledge of psychometric tests and assessment centres.

How do I feel about interviews?

Many people dread an interview, feeling as though it is a one-way process in which they are being interrogated and have no control over the situation. Changing the way you approach an interview changes the way you feel about it.

An interview is your opportunity to convince the employer that you are the right candidate for the job. Think of it as an exchange of information, an opportunity to talk about what you would bring to the role/organisation and how you could make a difference for them. You go to a job interview to discover whether your talents, abilities, interests and direction are a good fit for the job, the company and the organisation's mission.

When you have been selected for an interview, the employer will assume that you can do the job from having read your CV/application and your LinkedIn profile. However, for them to want to employ YOU, you must be able to demonstrate that you can do more than just how the job is described. The extra skills, experience, or talents that YOU bring to the job are your added value, and the interview is your chance to demonstrate what you could bring to the role/organisation that other candidates may not. You need to know what your added value is, and how to communicate it clearly.

It's all in the preparation

By looking ahead to the period immediately after an imaginary interview in which you have given the best possible account of yourself and your abilities, you can reflect on why you were successful, what you did well and how you were able to overcome the negative feelings identified in the previous exercise.

Envisioning is outcome-focused. By beginning with the end in mind, you can imagine your desired interview outcome and each of the steps that will lead you to it.

Psychometric tests

Psychometric tests help to identify your skills, knowledge and personality. They are often used during the preliminary screening stage, or as part of an assessment centre. Recruiters see them as objective, convenient and strong indicators of job performance – making them very popular with large employers.

There are two main types: personality tests and aptitude tests.

Personality tests

Personality tests explore your values, interests and motivations, assessing how your character fits with the role and organisation. They analyse your emotions, behaviours and relationships in a variety of situations.

Aptitude tests

Aptitude tests assess your reasoning or cognitive ability, determining whether you have the right skillset for a role. You'll often be given one minute to answer each multiple-choice question. Your intelligence levels are compared to a standard, meaning that you must achieve a certain score to pass. Common tests include:

- verbal reasoning
- diagrammatic reasoning
- error checking
- numerical reasoning
- spatial reasoning.

There are several places online where you can practice psycho-metric tests. Here is one option: https://www.jobtestprep.co.uk/free-psychometric-test

Assessment centres

An assessment centre is a recruitment selection process in which the organisation typically assesses a group of candidates at the same time using a range of selection exercises. Recruiters see assessment centres as one of the most effective methods for predicting a candidate's suit-ability for a job, helping to avoid poor recruitment decisions and the associated costs .

Assessment centres are relevant to the competencies of the role for which you are applying.

Tasks could include presentations, role-play, group discussions and written case studies. There may be an informal element of networking and socialising.

◆ **Know what to expect**
Thoroughly read the invitation to the assessment centre and prepare accordingly. For example, you may be asked to prepare a presentation in advance.

◆ **Research**
Research the role and organisation.

◆ **Review your application**
Make sure you know your CV/application inside out, as they are likely to ask you questions about this.

◆ **Check the key competencies**
Prepare specific STAR examples for each of the competencies.

◆ **Perfect your presentation**
Rehearse, rehearse, rehearse so you know it inside out.

◆ **Practice aptitude tests**
Check what sorts of tests may be given, then research and practice similar tests.

◆ **Interview practice**
There may be an element of an interview, so ensure that you know your STAR examples and have practiced them.

EXERCISES

Exercise 1 – How do you feel about interviews?

Write down, or tell a trusted friend or professional coach, your thoughts and feelings about attending interviews. If there are any feelings of nerves, fear, etc, identify what lies beneath them. What are you fearful/nervous about?

Do these feelings work in your favour or against you while you are preparing for and being interviewed?

Are your talents, abilities, interests and direction a good fit for the job, the company and the company's mission?

How can you demonstrate your added value?

What will help you keep calm on the day?

How to survive a job interview when you haven't had one for years

I had only ever been to two job interviews (the last one a casual chat eight years prior) when I turned up to a huge glass building in the city of London for an interview.

I was nervous and I don't have the cure for that. However, I do have some tips on how I managed to make it easier:

1. **Dress rehearsal**
   The "dress rehearsal" I'd done the week before was a godsend, as I knew how long it would take me and that there was a coffee shop next door where I could go to the loo and check out my appearance before I went in.

2. **Be careful what you eat and drink**
   I didn't get a coffee, as it makes me jittery. Instead, I opted for water, almonds and a banana, which I'd read contains calming beta-blockers. I also got some Rescue Remedy drops in the hope that it would keep the nerves at bay.

3. **Practice, practice, practice**
   I was so pleased that I'd practiced variations of the different possible interview topics, as this helped me keep calm and treat it as a conversation rather than an interrogation.

4. **Do your research**
   I knew lots about the organisation. To get some inside info, I went out of my way to speak to someone who knew of someone who worked there. I'd read the websites and Googled the organisation's name to see what articles came up. I knew role-specific knowledge, such as the governance of the organisation. I was prepared and had some suggestions for improvements.

5. **Breathe deeply and get rid of nervous energy**
   I did a run and some meditation that morning to get rid of nervous energy and get me in a good space.
   There were several lifts, none of which I could get

working to get to the sixth floor for my interview! I took deep breaths and asked someone for help.

6. **Reward yourself**

I did it! I was proud that I'd faced my fears and expanded my comfort zone in the process. I went to a friend's for dinner afterwards so I didn't go over all of the "if only I'd said…".

I got the job!

Joanna Lott

Exercise 2 – Creating a model of an excellent interview

What does a successful interview look like?

What do you have to do before, during, and after the interview to improve your chances of getting a job offer?

For this exercise, we will use the outcome-focused technique of envisioning.

Take some time to envisage the entire interview process, starting from immediately after the interview… to the closing section with questions to the interviewer… to the main interview… to the opening few minutes… to your arrival and waiting at reception… to your journey to the interview.

Unpicking the interview in this way enables you to isolate, analyse and address each stage and take control of it.

Ask a friend or professional coach to run through a practice interview with you. Then complete the exercise below on what you should be doing to excel at the interview.

Creating a model of an excellent Interview

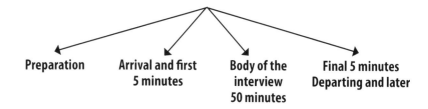

Preparation	Arrival and first 5 minutes	Body of the interview 50 minutes	Final 5 minutes Departing and later
Preparing in the days leading up to the interview	Arriving at the location and the first 5 minutes	During the body of the interview (approx 50 minutes)	Final 5 minutes of the interview, saying "goodbye", leaving the building and next day

Exercise 3 – Practice interview

Google "top interviewing questions" for your role and prepare your answers using the STAR technique as appropriate.

In the case of any "difficult questions", reframe them in your mind to make them "interesting questions".

Keep in mind that you are also interviewing them.

Ask a trusted friend or professional coach to hold a practice interview with you and provide them with the following guidelines.

Guidelines for a coach/friend conducting a practice interview

Before starting, review the job applicant's CV and either the job description of the role they have applied for or one that fits the kind of role they are seeking.

Where should the practice interview take place? Wherever possible, conduct the interview in the type of environment in which the interview is likely to take place.

How should the interview be structured? Allow 30 minutes for the practice interview. Greet the candidate and introduce yourself in the usual way, but move on to the interview fairly quickly.

What questions should I ask? Wherever possible, tailor your questions to the CV/job description provided before the interview. Vary the style of questioning to give the candidate the chance to answer both general (eg tell me about yourself) and specific (eg tell me about a time when…) questions.

Always include the question: "Is there anything you would like to ask me?" Even though you won't be able to answer them if they are company/job-specific, you will be able to provide useful feedback on the questions they have prepared to ask a potential interviewer.

How challenging should I be? The purpose of practice interviews is to make candidates feel more comfortable with the interview process and to identify areas where they could improve in order to present themselves more confidently. Don't make the practice interviews too easy, as this will not provide them with a realistic experience. Try to strike a balance between testing the limits of the candidate's capabilities and ability to respond well when put under pressure and not sending them into a panic.

When preparing suitable questions, consider the type of role for which the candidate is applying. If a candidate begins to struggle, provide a hint or switch to an alternative topic or line of questioning.

What feedback should I provide? Take notes throughout the interview to make the experience as realistic as possible and to use in your feedback. Providing constructive feedback will help the candidate identify which aspects of being interviewed s/he could improve upon. Use the following guidelines.

General
Feedback should be:

- Descriptive rather than subjective – describe what the candidate said or did and the impact that had on you, but do not make judgements.
- Specific rather than general – provide actual examples.
- Sensitively delivered – give equal time to identifying both strengths and weaknesses. Focus on aspects where the applicant can improve, suggesting practical ways for them to present themselves more favourably and rectify any shortcomings.
- Clearly and precisely stated – avoid beating around the bush but deliver feedback with consideration.

Meeting and greeting

◆ What was your first impression of the candidate? Was s/he dressed appropriately for the kind of job for which s/he was being interviewed?

◆ How did the candidate come across in the first few minutes? Handshake, eye contact, confidence, etc.

During the practice interview

◆ General communication and non-verbal cues
  ■ confidence, poise, smile, eye contact, nervous fidgeting?
  ■ body language and enthusiasm
  ■ ability to hear and understand the candidate – did s/he speak easily and clearly and at a comfortable pace?

◆ Responses
  ■ Did the candidate always answer the questions or were there occasions when s/he switched to prepared statements unrelated to the questions asked or drifted onto another subject?
  ■ How well did the candidate use accomplishments and achievements to provide examples of important skills?
  ■ How well did the candidate turn any questions addressing weaknesses into positives?

Post-interview feedback

◆ Discuss the candidate's manner and behaviour when giving constructive feedback.
  ■ Be specific, clear and descriptive, giving concrete examples.
  ■ Identify positive aspects first – what s/he did well. Then identify areas for possible improvement and change.

◆ Questions to consider when providing constructive feedback:

- Did the candidate provide satisfactory answers to all your questions? If not, be specific about which ones and why.
- Did s/he appear to undersell or exaggerate his/her skills, abilities, or experience?
- Was your first impression of the candidate confirmed or contradicted in the interview?
- Would you remember the candidate? (For the right reasons!)
- Would you employ the candidate?

◆ Ensure the applicant understands the feedback by asking them questions and summarising. If time permits, allow the candidate to recap areas for improvement and what they have taken away from the practice interview. Always end on a positive and encouraging note.

Useful resources

Books

◆ *Answering Tough Interview Questions For Dummies* by Rob Yeung; John Wiley and Sons

◆ *Great Answers to Tough Interview Questions* by Martin John Yate; Kogan Page.

Websites

◆ https://www.assessmentday.co.uk/video-interviews.htm – video interview practice tips

◆ https://www.assessmentday.co.uk/competency-based-interview.htm – example interview questions.

Chapter 9

Presenting well at interviews

"A man cannot be comfortable without his own approval."

—Mark Twain

Learning outcomes

By the end of this chapter you will:

- know a set of "model" answers to common interview questions
- appreciate how to ask good questions yourself
- feel confident to make an interview a two-way process.

What's behind the question?

By the time you get to an interview, you will meet the person specification more or less. Your CV/application will have demonstrated that you appear to have the skills to do the job, so the purpose of the interview is to find out the answers to three questions:

- **How well can you do the job?** Do you have the knowledge, skills, strengths and competencies to carry out the job to the standard required?
- **Will you do the job?** What is your motivation for wanting to do this job in this organisation?
- **Will you fit in?** Will you get along with the organisation, the team and the way things are done here?

Types of questions you may be asked

Under the exercises in this chapter, we will look at the types of questions you may be asked and work on preparing answers in each category:

- about you – background, skills and experience
- about your work/career history
- about the new job and organisation
- about the future, your educational background, salary expectations, etc.

Do you have any questions for me? Your chance to stand out

This is your chance to shine. An interviewer often ends by asking the candidate if they have any questions. However, if you ask questions throughout the interview rather than just at the end, it leads to a more interactive exchange and makes the whole process feel less like a one-way street. If it feels appropriate, ask as you go along, as and when you are talking about a relevant topic. Make sure the interviewer is comfortable with that approach; always check if you are not sure.

Asking the right questions serves several purposes. Firstly, it helps you to determine whether or not you are qualified for the job, would be able to do it and actually want the role. Is this the right job/ organisation for you?

Secondly, asking a few good questions can impress the interviewer and help convince them that you're the person for the job. Always ask questions that are relevant to the job and to the opportunity with which you are being presented.

Online interviews

Many interviews now take place online. It is important to note that:

1. **Standard rules still apply**
   You should dress appropriately, including shoes. This can have an important psychological effect on you.

2. **Minimise distractions**
   Turn off your mobile phone and TV. Close down all browsers on your computer so you don't receive any distracting pop-up messages.

3. **Make sure you are in a quiet place**
   Ask your family members to go out for a while, if possible.

4. **Consider your background**
   Go for as neutral as possible, ensuring there is no washing or untidiness in the background.

5. **Where's the light?**
   The window should be in front of you where possible. Check out the lighting beforehand to ensure that you can be seen clearly.

◆ **Look at the camera**
   Look at the camera as much as you can, rather than only the screen, to connect with your interviewer. You can put

a Post-it note on the screen to remind you. You can also use one to cover your own face on the screen if you find seeing yourself distracting. Some programmes such as Zoom enable you to hide your face from yourself.

6. **Test the software**
Ensure that you have the right software and test it in advance.

7. **Practice**
Software such as Zoom allows you to record yourself so that you can practice and watch back ahead of the real interview.

8. **Notes**
Note down and keep a few key bullet points close by, where the interviewer can't see them, to prompt your thinking. This is where being online can be helpful.

Top tips on making a presentation

Remember that the main purpose of an interview, including any presentation, is for the interviewers to:

◆ ascertain how well you would fit in with the organisation, especially the team you would be joining, and with its clients
◆ clarify any points that are unclear in your CV by asking for practical examples.

You will be assessing whether you would like to join and would feel happy in this organisation.

Planning

- Find out how many people will be on the interview panel, including their names and job titles and the expected length of your presentation (excluding time for questions)

- If possible arrange to see the interview room beforehand – eg, if you are going for an in-house promotion. Check the layout and lighting and locate the nearest mains socket points.

- Assuming a 15- to 20-minute presentation, decide on the three main points you want to get across, eg, the top three requirements in the job description. Do not introduce other material, as it will detract from your main messages.

- Structure your talk
  - strong opening – attention-grabber covering **why** you've chosen this topic / recommendation
  - the main content
    - **what** is your solution
    - **how** you are going to make it happen
    - **who** will be involved
  - conclusion, with a strong ending
    - **when** will this happen
  - a case study in the STAR format
  - thank the panellists for listening attentively
  - hand back to the person leading the interview.

- Use visual aids sparingly
  - Ensure the slides are visually attractive and not just a prop for you.
  - Make sure your slides aren't too text-heavy and consider using the same font as that used by the panellists' company

- Choose a large font size and dense, dark colours (red and yellow do not carry well to the back of a large room).
- Use research from industry leaders and make sure you include any references for third-party sources.
- Rehearse, rehearse, rehearse in front of family members and friends. Check that the sequence of your talk flows naturally. Rehearsing will increase your self-confidence.
- Take your own laptop and audiovisual equipment to the interview.

The presentation itself

- If you are asked to give a 30- to 45-minute presentation, hand out a skeleton outline of it before you start.
- Thank the panellists for inviting you to the interview and for the opportunity to give your presentation.
- Agree with the panellists on whether questions should be saved until the end of your presentation (a better option for you) or raised as you go through the talk.
- Speak with enthusiasm and from the heart. "Enthusiasm is contagious." This is at least as important as your content. As Maya Angelou said: "People don't remember what you said or even what you did, but they always remember how you made them feel."
- You will come across well if you demonstrate, through the energy in your voice, your enthusiasm about the organisation and the opportunity the vacancy offers you.
- Maintain a steady speed of voice and vary the pitch.
- Make an equal amount of eye contact with all the panel members.
- Manage your hand movements and any mannerisms you have.

◆ Speak sincerely, without exaggerating your skills or achievements.

Answering questions

◆ Keep your laptop open, as a questioner may ask you to clarify an earlier slide.

◆ Panel members are not going to try to trick you or catch you out, so welcome questions.

◆ Where appropriate, check that you have understood a question before you answer it.

◆ Try and use brief STAR-type stories to give examples of a skill and, as always, focus on the outcome/result.

◆ Use the first person, eg, "I decided to…". rather than "We….".

◆ Check that the questioner is happy with your answer.

◆ If you have not had the exact experience that the panellist is asking you about, give an equivalent answer, eg, "No, I haven't worked with German clients but I have worked with Dutch and Italian clients and visited those countries."

◆ If you do not know the answer to a question, say so and offer to find out after the interview. Then get back to them with an answer.

◆ At the end, thank them for their questions.

Talking money

You will need to talk about money at some stage but ideally not until you are in a position to negotiate, ie, when they have already offered you the job. We will run through some pointers on this in the exercises.

EXERCISES

Exercise 1 – What's behind the question?

There are four different question categories. Work through a number of the questions, identifying what you perceive to be the *real* question in each case. What is the interviewer trying to find out? With this in mind, prepare some model answers to as many of the questions as possible. Use your own STARs when preparing answers to the "tell me about a time when…" type of questions.

- ◆ questions about you – background, skills, and experience
- ◆ questions about your work/career history
- ◆ questions about the new job and organisation
- ◆ questions about the future and your educational background, salary expectations, etc.

Behavioural questions

- ◆ Give an example of a problem that you have had to solve. What did you do and what was the outcome?
- ◆ Give an example of a target you achieved and tell me how you went about it.
- ◆ Give an example of how you set goals and how you would go about achieving them.
- ◆ Give an example of a goal you didn't meet and how you handled it.
- ◆ Describe a difficult situation at work and how you handled it.
- ◆ How do you deal with a challenge that you have not faced before?
- ◆ Tell me about a time when you had to work under pressure. How did you handle it?

◆ Tell me about a time when you had to work on a number of projects. How did you prioritise?

◆ Have you ever made a mistake at work? How did you handle it and what was the outcome?

◆ Tell me about a decision that you made which was unpopular. How did you implement it?

◆ Have you ever dealt with a company policy that you didn't agree with? What did you do?

◆ Give an example of when you worked on a successful team. What was your contribution? What made the team successful?

◆ Have you handled a difficult situation with a manager/client/colleague? How?

◆ What would you do if you disagreed with your manager about an important issue at work?

Questions about the new job and the organisation

◆ Why do you want this job or what interests you about this job?

◆ Why do you think you are suitable (or the best candidate) for this job?

◆ Do you think you are overqualified for this job?

◆ What would you bring to this job/organisation? What can you contribute?

◆ What do you know about this organisation?

◆ Do you prefer to work in a small, medium or large company?

◆ What would your ideal job be?

◆ Are you considering any other positions at the moment?

◆ Have you ever been fired?

◆ How often are you off sick?

◆ What will your referees say about you?

- Why do you want to work here?
- What do you think the main challenges will be in this role?
- What would you do in the first day/week/month/year?
- How long do you anticipate working for this organisation?
- What do you know about/think about our products/services?
- Do you have any suggestions on how we could improve our products/services?

Questions about the future

- What are you looking for in your next job? What is important to you?
- What are your career or life goals for the next five years/10 years?
- How do you plan to achieve those goals?

Questions about you

- Tell me about yourself.
- How would you describe yourself?
- Please describe a typical working week.
- How would you describe your work style?
- What are your strengths/weaknesses?
- Where do you see yourself in five and 10 years' time?
- What are your short-term and long-term goals in life?
- What motivates you?
- Which tasks do you get the most satisfaction from?
- How do you define/measure success?
- Why should we hire you?
- Why do you think you would do well in this job?
- What are you passionate about?
- What is your philosophy towards work?
- Do you ever take work home with you?

- What is a normal working week for you? How many hours do you work?
- How well do you work under pressure? How do you handle stress? Give me an example of when you have had to work under pressure. How did you handle it?
- Describe a situation in which you could not resolve a problem.
- What decisions do you find the most difficult to make?
- What would your last manager say about you?
- If the people who know you were asked why you should be hired, what would they say?
- Do you prefer to work independently or on a team?
- Give me an example of when you have been part of a team that worked well together. What was your role and what did you do to contribute to the team's success?
- What do you think are the most important elements of teamwork?

Work history

- What have you been doing since your last job?
- What were your responsibilities in your last job?
- What did you like or dislike most about your previous job?
- Which aspect of your last job was most/least rewarding?
- What challenges and problems did you face? How did you handle them?
- What was your most successful accomplishment in your last position?
- What was your biggest mistake/failure and how did you handle it?
- What have you learned from past mistakes?
- What was your last manager like and what was it like working for him/her?

- What do you expect from a manager or supervisor?
- Have you ever had any problems working with a manager? How did you deal with him/her?
- In previous roles that you have held, who was your best manager and what was it about him/her that you liked?
- Who was your worst manager and why?

Exercise 2 – Do you have any questions you'd like to ask me? Your chance to stand out

Asking the right questions serves a number of purposes. Firstly, it helps you determine whether you are qualified for the job, would be able to do it and actually want the role you are being interviewed for. Is it the right job/organisation for you?

Secondly, asking a few good questions can make a strong impression on the interviewer, and help convince him/her that you're the person for the job. Always ask questions that are relevant to the job and to the opportunity with which you are being presented.

TOP TIP

Don't ask how much holiday or sickness entitlement you'll have! That just shows you're interested in not being there…

Do ask:

- about the job in more detail
- about the rest of the team you will work with
- about any issues you should be aware of between team members
- about the boss – what is s/he like to work for?
- about the company and its expansion/strategic plans
- about the prospects (but only if that genuinely matters to you)

- ◆ about what you will have achieved in the first six months/ year to prove that you are the right person for the job.

But don't ask too many questions, as the interviewers may be on a tight schedule.

Questions should be written out and taken with you so that you can demonstrate your preparation in case they have told you absolutely everything during the interview.

Exercise 3 – Talking money

You will need to talk about money at some stage but ideally not until you are in a position to negotiate, ie, when they have already offered you the job. That makes these sorts of questions doubly difficult...

- ◆ What's your current salary?
- ◆ What's your current package?
- ◆ What salary are you looking for?

Once prospective employers know what you've earned in previous positions, they may use that information to decide how to pitch the salary – sufficiently high to attract you but not more than they need to pay to get you.

This can make it difficult to negotiate a salary that truly reflects your talent and value. What if your previous position was underpaid? You don't want to perpetuate that, do you? And if asked to say how much you want to earn, you are caught between the danger of overpricing yourself and underpricing yourself.

Tips for money talk

Never volunteer your salary details unless you are expecting a broadly comparable salary and do not intend to negotiate.

- Talk in "broad package" or "circa" terms to give you the maximum room for manoeuvring.
- Try to avoid the question about salary requirements by saying: "At this stage, money is not the most important factor to me. I would much rather concentrate on understanding the job and what exactly you are looking for…" or "I am looking for a fair market salary for this type of work."
- Be prepared to indicate your salary requirement if you have to, but make sure you have done some research first.
- Know your facts – what sorts of salaries are paid for jobs like this, in organisations like this?
- State a range, not a single figure – possibly indicating a minimum acceptable and a desired figure.
- If you think you are "overpaid" for a job for which you are being interviewed, you could say: "As I am changing sector/ career to one in which I have considerably less experience, I am not expecting to earn the same salary. Therefore, I don't think my current salary is particularly relevant."
- If you are pressed for your current salary and don't wish to give it, perhaps because you think you may be underpaid currently, you could try: "I don't feel my current salary is a good indicator of what I should earn in a future role, as the sectors are so different" or "I am/was significantly underpaid in my current/last position and I'm looking for a fair market salary for this position."

Exercise 4 – Ending the interview well

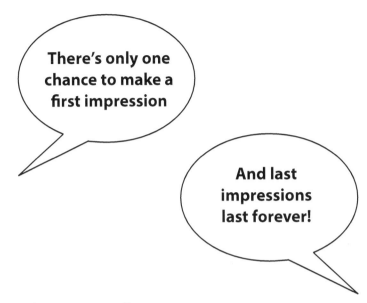

There's only one chance to make a first impression

And last impressions last forever!

Some ideas for endings...

- "I am confident I can do a really good job for you in this role. Do you have any areas of doubt?"
- "I am very keen to progress further but do have a couple of other job applications in train. This job is definitely at the top of my list so could you tell me how soon you can let me know your final decision?"
- "Thank you very much for your time. I have found the interview very interesting and feel really enthusiastic about the job. I'm looking forward to hearing from you soon."

Useful resources

Covered in the previous chapter but there are many more resources online.

Chapter 10

Support systems and next steps

"Alone we can do so little, together we can do so much."

—Helen Keller

Learning outcomes

By the end of this chapter you will:

◆ understand how to put support systems in place
◆ have a set of short-term goals and an action plan to achieve them.

Your story so far – reflecting on what you have learnt

Life is a journey and your job search is a journey. You do not need to make the journey alone – even if you live alone, or are a long way (physically, emotionally, etc) from family or friends. There are communities of support out there. In this chapter, we will look at the next steps you need to take along your personal journey and what support is available.

Where are you? Where have you come from and what have you achieved?

It is important to reflect on where you have come from and what you have already achieved.

Where are you going? Take stock and plan the next steps

You are 42% more likely to reach your goal if you write it down – that percentage rises dramatically when you share your goal and as high as 95% if you have an accountability partner. Consider your goals for the next few days/weeks/months.

What difference will it make?

This step will see that you recognise the benefits of achieving the goals you have set for yourself to assist with momentum.

Getting started

Put it into practice by developing an action plan, step by step.

EXERCISES

Exercise 1 – Your story so far

If possible, work with a trusted friend or coach to:

- ◆ introduce yourself using your Elevator Pitch
- ◆ share something of your journey since you started this toolkit (what you have learned, what you do differently now, how you have changed, eg, increased confidence, etc)
- ◆ share some of the good things that have happened to you recently (drawing from your gratitude journal).

Exercise 2 – Where are you? Taking stock and planning next steps

In this chart below, complete the first box – "My current position" – as fully as possible. You should include what you have already achieved and what is still outstanding on your Career Planning System.

Reflect on how feel about your achievements, looking back over the period you have been working through the toolkit.

Is there still more to work on? New things to learn, new people to meet, new strategies to try?

MY CURRENT POSITION	BY --/--/---- I SPECIFICALLY WANT TO...	BENEFITS OF ACHIEVING MY GOAL ARE:

"No matter how carefully you plan your goals, they will never be more than pipe dreams unless you pursue them with gusto."
W. Clement Stone

"Planning is bringing the future into the present so that you can do something about it now."
Alan Lakein

Exercise 3 – Next steps action plan

Let's break it down into actionable steps. Complete the form below:

TASK	FIRST STEPS IN DETAIL	END DATE	SUPPORT NEEDED	SUCCESSFUL IF...

Useful resources

Websites

- https://careerattraction.com/goal-setting-for-a-successful-job-search/ – goal setting for a successful job search
- http://www.jobseekersguide.org/make-your-goal-setting-plan – make your goal setting plan

Chapter 11

Is self-employment for me?

"It is better to have enough ideas for some of them to be wrong, than to be always right by having no ideas at all."

—Edward de Bono

Learning outcomes

By the end of this chapter you will:

- ◆ be able to decide if self-employment is for you
- ◆ understand the main tasks you should complete before you launch your business
- ◆ be prepared for the questions a business adviser may ask you.

Is self-employment for me?

Most of the ground covered in previous chapters have assumed that you are seeking work as an employee within an organisation (business, charity, public sector, etc).

While it is outside the scope of this book to cover self-employment in detail, this chapter will help you decide if this option is worth exploring, even if you have not considered it before.

The pros and cons of self-employment

The pros may include:

- ◆ reaping the rewards of your own efforts – the reward is more proportional to the effort
- ◆ chance to do something you love and are passionate about – increased job satisfaction and sense of fulfilment
- ◆ more freedom/flexibility regarding working hours – control of your time
- ◆ quality of life – working close to home, less time travelling
- ◆ cutting costs and hassle regarding commuting, traffic congestion, etc.

The cons may include:

- ◆ sole responsibility – the buck stops with you; everything is down to you
- ◆ no "corporate benefits", eg, sick pay, maternity pay, paid holidays, etc
- ◆ lower income initially
- ◆ the responsibility of employing others
- ◆ Having to do your own marketing and selling, accounts/taxes/pensions, etc.
- ◆ missing being part of a team, maybe feeling isolated
- ◆ initially less time with family, working long hours to establish the business
- ◆ needing capital to set up and worrying about future cash flow.

Character traits and skills

The character traits you need will include:

◆ drive and determination
◆ a clear focus on your goals
◆ marketing and selling skills
◆ willingness to learn
◆ hard work
◆ infectious enthusiasm for your idea
◆ common sense and realism
◆ ability to create rapport and trust with potential clients.

Skills are likely to include technical skills and knowledge about your product/service, etc, project planning and delivery, IT skills (including social media, marketing, and selling), business skills and financial skills (especially in fixing your selling prices, terms of service, cash flow, etc.).

You may not be fully competent in all the above. In that case, you could go into business with a trusted friend with complementary skills, or pay for external support, or learn about the ones you lack, eg, social media or selling.

EXERCISES

Exercise 1 – Self-employment questions to ask yourself

Questions	Your comments
Why do I want to start my own business? What are the key drivers behind my being self-employed?	
What do I want to gain, personally and professionally? What will the benefits be?	
What do I know about starting a business? What reading, research or learning do I need to do? Who can I talk to?	
What business skills, financial resources and personal support do I need to make a new business a success?	
Do I have all these, and if not, how could I get them?	
What are my greatest skills and strengths?	
What are my greatest limitations? Would these prevent me from being successfully self-employed?	
Will I enjoy running my own business? Will I enjoy the lifestyle?	

Questions	Your comments
Will the daily activities and challenges satisfy me? Am I prepared for the responsibility that is involved (to myself, my family, my employees)?	
What will a typical day look like? A typical week? Will I have time for other things that are important to me?	
What impact might this career change have on relationships with my family and friends?	
Am I at the right stage of my life to pursue self-employment?	

Exercise 2 – Preparing a business plan

You should prepare a business plan covering the five areas in the next section. If you do not need additional funding, your plan needs to be only two or three pages, plus a cash flow projection.

A more sophisticated and longer plan and financial projections are required if you need external funding. Your accountant should be able to explain what the plan and financial projections should cover, including a one-page executive summary, or you can base it on the detailed points in the next section.

We recommend that you write the plan yourself so as to be better placed when answering questions about it. You may need help completing the financial projections, including the written assumptions on which the financial projections are based.

The five "Vs", where v stands for viability

When you are discussing your business plan, eg, with a business advisor or investor, they are likely to ask questions about the viability of your product or service, marketing and sales, management, methods of operating and financial control.

Viability of...	Your response
Product or service Is your product or service finished? Do you own it? Has it been tested? Are you sticking to this product or service or are you already thinking of revising/changing it? Will you be using external suppliers/sub-contractors?	
Marketing and sales What is your USP (unique selling point or proposition)? What is your target market? What geographical area(s) will you be covering? How many customers have already purchased from you? What is the value of firm orders you have received? How are you promoting your company? What other effective methods are you considering? Are you selling through an intermediary or direct? Do you have a detailed marketing plan? Who are your direct/indirect competitors? In what ways are you using networking?	

Viability of...	Your response
Management What management experience do you have? What aspect of management do you enjoy most? Least? How are you feeling about being self-employed? Who owns the business? Is it a partnership, sole trader or limited company? Are you planning to employ staff or use sub-contractors? Do you have written terms of service for use with, for example, sub-contractors and customers? What professional advisors, eg, lawyers, are you using? Do you have a support group of trusted friends? Which professional groups are you a member of?	
Methods of operating What is the purpose of your website? What software and other systems are you using? Are all these working well? Can they cope with business expansion? Who will sort out system failures and how quickly? What premises do you operate from?	

Viability of...	Your response
Financial control What is your experience with book-keeping and financial control?	
Do you have a cash flow statement covering the next, say, 18 months, complete with your written assumptions?	
Where will additional cash come from to cover contingencies and business expansion?	
What accounting and management information system do you use?	
Have you opened a business bank account and registered your business with HMRC?	
With a rapidly expanding business, have you registered for VAT, perhaps voluntary registration?	

Useful resources

Websites

◆ https://www.gov.uk/set-up-business – government advice on setting up a business, including information about tax and VAT registration

Books

There are hundreds of books on starting your own business. Here are just a few:

◆ *Starting and Running a Business All-in-One for Dummies* by Colin Barrow; For Dummies

◆ *The Female Entrepreneur: A Step-by-Step Guide to the Adventure That Is Starting Your Own Business!* by Charly Lester and Caroline Brealey; independently published

◆ *Self-Made: The Definitive Guide to Business Start-Up Success* by Bianca Miller-Cole and Byron Cole; John Murray Learning.

Conclusion

What now?

We know that you want to get into a fulfilling job or career and we have created this toolkit to take you through those steps. For some people, particularly if they complete all the exercises, that will be enough.

Others may have become overwhelmed or stuck at some point, so they want additional help.

Further materials

We offer free exercises and resources on the co-author's website:

- www.joannalottcoaching.com

We add additional free materials regularly, so do keep an eye on the site.

Inspiration and content

For inspiration and further resources, you can connect with us on social media:

LinkedIn

◆ https://www.linkedin.com/in/joannalott/
◆ https://www.linkedin.com/in/richard-fox-a843272/

Instagram

◆ https://www.instagram.com/joanna_lott_coaching/

Career membership, group coaching programmes and one-to-one coaching

Your job search can be a worrying or lonely time, leaving you feeling anxious and overwhelmed as you consider where to start and how to maintain momentum. If you are job hunting by yourself and would like support, accountability and motivation along the way, we are creating group and one-to-one coaching programmes, based on the Career Planning System.

Our approach with group programmes is to build a community among the participants and provide additional learning, inspiration and support. You can learn more by visiting www.joannalottcoaching.com.

You can also join our free Facebook community, A Satisfied Mind – https://www.facebook.com/groups/asatisfiedmind

10 most useful additional resources

1. www.linkedin.com – best site for connecting with recruiters and professional networking
2. https://nationalcareers.service.gov.uk/ – information, advice, and guidance if you live in England to help you make decisions on learning, training, and work
3. https://linkedin.github.io/career-explorer/ – LinkedIn Career Explorer to find new jobs with the skills you already have
4. www.indeed.com – the largest job website
5. https://www.monster.com/ – caters to job seekers of all experience levels and work styles
6. www.glassdoor.com – bringing salary transparency and honest company reviews to millions of current and prospective employees; can also search for open jobs
7. www.flexjobs.com – remote, work from home and flexible job opportunities
8. https://angel.co/ – best for start-up jobs
9. www.theladders.com/ – best for high-paying managerial jobs
10. https://scouted.io/ – best for recent graduates

About the authors

Richard Fox

Richard' career is in two distinct parts. After university he became trained as a chartered accountant. He had unparalleled business experience covering all industry sectors except health. He advised companies in their different stages of development. He advised many start-ups, acquisitions, a flotation and the audit of global companies.

The second half of his career has been in the world of learning and development. He has worked with companies such as Syngenta, Canon, IBM, KPMG focusing on leadership at the personal, interpersonal and organisational levels.

During the last recession Richard, over a period of four years, co-facilitated the Guildford job club every Monday morning. The facilitator's guide he created has provided the majority of the content for this Toolkit.

Richard is author of three books "Creating a purposeful life", "Making Relationships work at work" (achieving the number one Amazon best-selling award) and has co-authored this Toolkit.

Richard can be contacted via rjfox@btinternet.com.

Joanna Lott

Joanna Lott is a post-graduate qualified Career and Executive Coach specialising in career transition. She writes about careers and living a purposeful life to support others in becoming the people they are here to be.

She is a qualified HR professional with experience in recruitment and 20 years' experience working within human resources, organisational development and governance for trade unions and financial services.

Joanna lives in Surrey with her husband and two children.

She would love to meet you at www.joannalottcoaching.com.

Printed in Great Britain
by Amazon